BLAIR'S WAR

BLAIR'S WAR

David Coates and Joel Krieger

(with Rhiannon Vickers)

polity

First published in 2004 by Polity Press Ltd.

Polity Press
65 Bridge Street
Cambridge CB2 1UR, UK

Polity Press
350 Main Street
Malden, MA 02148, USA

ISBN: 0-7456 3358-7
ISBN: 0-7456 3359-5 (paperback)

A catalogue record for this book is available from the British Library and
has been applied for from the Library of Congress.

Typeset in 10.5 on 12pt Sabon
by Graphicraft Limited, Hong Kong
Printed and bound in Great Britain by MPG Books, Bodmin, Cornwall

For further information on Polity, visit our website: www.polity.co.uk

Contents

'The absence of evidence is a bloody thin ground on
which to build a war.'

*Robin Cook, former UK Foreign Secretary, to the Foreign
Affairs Committee of the House of Commons, 24 June 2003*

'Last fall, the President said that Iraq was developing nuclear
weapons. Then, he said Iraq maintains an active weapons of mass
destruction program. Then, the rationale was that Iraq was linked
to Al Qaeda. None of these are true. No one doubts that Saddam
Hussein was an evil dictator, but what was the imminent threat
to our national security? The Administration's rationale was
built on a quicksand of false assumptions.'

Senator Edward Kennedy, to the US Senate, 23 September 2003

Acknowledgements

This was a war with unusual literary sensibilities. Its key participants have already decided how they intend to characterize the literature yet to be written upon it. So what follows is an early example of what George Bush has already labelled a 'revisionist history'. We also hope that it is an early example of what one witness before the Foreign Affairs Committee of the House of Commons called 'great books [that] will be written about this issue'. But great or not, in the writing of it we have accumulated many debts. The largest by far is to Rhiannon Vickers, who was an early joint architect of this scheme, the main writer of the material now in chapter 2, and a vital critic and adviser throughout the entire exercise. We are indebted too to Bob Woodward and Peter Stothard for two fascinating 'fly on the wall' reports on the policy process: one from inside the White House (Woodward's *Bush at War*); and one inside 10 Downing Street (Stothard's *30 Days: A Month at the Heart of Blair's War*). We have also amassed huge debts to three outstandingly able Wake Forest students (Elizabeth 'Nikki' Marterre, Ben Halfhill and Katherine Winstead) for their help in accumulating the speeches, testimony before Congressional Committees and evidence before Select Committees of the UK Parliament, on which our account heavily depends; and we have a much longer-term debt to Dr Gail Stedward for the ease of our access to UK newspaper reports and analyses. We are also indebted to Michaelle Browers and Charles Kennedy for the technical expertise, friendship and encouragement that they provided at key points in the production of this book; and to Leslie Gardner for her immense help in bringing the book to market. But our greatest debt, as ever, is to those who love us. Our families provided huge quantities of support and pleasure throughout the entire research and writing exercise, and for that there can be no thanks great enough. Indeed, since this book has been written in the hope of shaping the future as well as of recording the past, it is only right and proper that it is to the junior members of those families that it should be dedicated. No dedication was ever easier to conjure up and to give.

This one is for Jonathan, Nathan and Megan.

It comes with love.

David Coates and Joel Krieger

The Problem of Blair's War

In most wars the principle holds: to the victor go the spoils. But that was not the case in this war. The invasion of Iraq was a short affair, and in military terms an unambiguously successful one. The first sustained air bombardment began on 20 March 2003, and the ground offensive a day later. By 1 May George Bush was able to stand on the deck of the *USS Abraham Lincoln* and declare that major combat operations in Iraq had ended. Wars hardly come shorter and more successful than this.

Yet a mere three months later, the political honeymoon created for both George Bush and Tony Blair by that rapid military success was visibly gone. The heady atmosphere of success was already long gone in London, and it was beginning quickly to dissipate in Washington. By the middle of 2003 both the President and the Prime Minister found themselves under heavy and regular pressure to justify the war they had won. Both men found themselves facing repeated calls to explain why they had taken their countries to war; and both found themselves obliged to defend the justifications they had used earlier to do so. The list of woes faced by the victors mounted rapidly.

In the USA, the steady drip, drip, drip of returning military body bags (52 in the first three post-war months alone) rapidly corroded the President's standing in the opinion polls, by raising in wider and wider sections of the US electorate the fear of another 'quagmire' like Vietnam: of a distant war with no exit strategy in sight. Those fears were then compounded by the Administration's inability through the autumn of 2003 to persuade more than a token number of countries to send troops to Iraq to assist in 'post-war reconstruction'. By late September, indeed, the US Administration was talking openly of its need to deploy more part-time soldiers (National Guard and Army reserve troops) in Iraq to make up for this international shortfall; and across the US population as a whole the popularity of its war began to decline commensurately.

This growing US unease about long-term troop deployments was by then being compounded on a daily basis by reports of anti-American demonstrations and ambushes in Iraq itself – news stories that made clear the degree of popular resistance within Iraq to an externally imposed 'liberation' that had earlier been projected by the White House as likely to be both rapidly accomplished and universally welcomed. Even more troubling for the Administration was the fact that this growing US unease was not restricted to the families of the men and women serving in Iraq. It was evident among the troops themselves: to such a point indeed that by July the US and UK media were openly reporting an unprecedented outburst of protest from US soldiers, angry that they were being ordered to police an increasingly dangerous Iraq rather than rapidly to return home, as they had been led to believe would be their fate.[1]

By then, in any case, the credibility of the whole exercise was being brought into wider and wider disrepute by the prolonged inability of US and UK forces to find any weapons of mass destruction in the Iraq they now controlled, and by the way in which the reliability of key pieces of evidence once used to sustain the case for war was now being brought into question. So, for example, the claim that the Iraqi Government had sought to develop nuclear weapons by seeking uranium in Niger – evidence which had been presented as 'hard' and 'totally reliable' as recently as in the President's 2003 State of the Union Address – was by July being dismissed as unambiguously false: and recognized as such by the White House itself.[2] Likewise, and in the same month, the second dossier of evidence on the threat to global security published by the Blair Government – a dossier hurriedly issued in February 2003 to bolster the fragile UK public support for unilateral military action – was now dismissed, even by the Foreign Secretary whose department had issued it, as 'the dodgy dossier ... [and] a complete horlicks'.[3] And then, to cap it all, in October the interim report of the Iraq Survey Group on the post-war search for weapons of mass destruction in Iraq very strongly suggested that no such weapons had existed immediately prior to the invasion whose prime legitimation had been their impending deployment by Saddam Hussein.[4]

Not surprisingly, then, popular support for the war and its architects also slipped away, as month followed month, in the UK as well as in the USA; and that erosion was compounded – in the UK case – by the way in which the Government there had allowed itself to become embroiled in a bitter and prolonged public row with the BBC: over the Corporation's claim that it (in the person of the Prime Minister's official spokesman) had 'sexed up' its original (September 2002) dossier of evidence on Iraq's chemical, biological and nuclear arsenal and potential. That public row triggered both a Select Committee Report into the BBC's claim and a judicial inquiry into the subsequent apparent suicide of the scientist who had been the BBC's prime source for the story: all of which kept the issue of the Government's credibility in relation to Iraq in the forefront of political debate in the UK right through the summer of 2003, and ate away at New Labour's standing in the opinion polls. The Hutton investigation proved particularly damaging in this regard: not least by making it clear that, even if the September dossier had not been directly tampered with, it had nonetheless been issued by a government aware that at least some of its intelligence data was less reliable than was initially claimed. So by the time the inquiry was over, and even before its report was issued, public opinion in the UK had switched decisively *against* the war. In the immediate wake of the war in April, public support for it in the UK had peaked at 63 per cent. But by August half the UK electorate was already convinced that the Government had embellished the case for war; and by September a clear majority of those questioned (58 per cent) replied that they now thought the war to have been unjustified, with only 38 per cent reporting that they now thought that the invasion of Iraq had been the right thing to do.[5]

Finally, in this catalogue of woes, the regular evidence of ongoing 'terrorist attacks' on US targets and allies overseas continued to place a huge question-mark over the credibility of the biggest of all the claims made for the war: the one that said that, by invading Iraq, the Bush Administration and its UK allies had actually advanced the security of the western democracies. There was a spate of such attacks in May – on targets in Saudi Arabia, Morocco and Israel – but though they then abated through the summer, the popular expectation that there would be more did not. When ABC News surveyed the US population in April 2003, they found that 58 per cent of those questioned thought that the war had reduced the danger of a further terrorist attack on the USA, and only 29 per cent thought that it had made domestic terrorism more likely. But by September those figures had reversed: 40 per cent feeling they were safer, 48 per cent that they were not. For by then other opinion polls were reporting that almost two-thirds of the US population now believed that a US military presence in the Middle East increased the likelihood of terrorism at home, and the Bush Administration itself was on record as expecting another major al-Qaeda attack.[6]

In both capitals, therefore, by the summer of 2003, leading Government figures were being regularly called upon to do some or all of a series of things. They were being called upon to justify the war and its outcome; they were being called upon to defend their previous justifications of the war; and they were being exposed to accusations of inconsistency, lack of clarity or worse, even on occasion to calls for their resignation. Those calls were initially quite muted; and they remained so, in the United States at least, through the autumn of 2003. There was a call in Washington, as early as July, for the Vice-President to resign – made by a group of former senior intelligence officers angry at the selective use of intelligence data in the presentation of the case for war;[7] and the possibility of presidential impeachment on similar grounds was then floated by at least one of the senators seeking the Democratic Party nomination for the presidential election of 2004.[8] But the real pressure for resignation came in London, not in Washington; and it came on Tony Blair, not on George Bush. Clare Short was initially a lone voice making that call. She made it regularly after resigning from the Government in May; but by September she was alone no longer. For, as the Labour Party gathered for its annual conference, fully a quarter of the backbench MPs polled were of the view that Tony Blair should immediately resign, and another 25 per cent thought that he should go either just before or just after the next general election.[9] And in holding to those views, the MPs were by then at one with 50 per cent of the public polled by MORI for the *Financial Times*, who also thought that, because of the illegitimacy of arguments used to justify the Iraq war, the Prime Minister should now resign.[10]

That drift of opinion, within and beyond the Labour Party, was fuelled by at least two linked sets of concerns. One – a set of concerns about the legitimacy of the arguments used to justify the war – eroded public trust in political leadership on both sides of the Atlantic; but the other – concerns about the subordination of UK policy to Washington – was unique to London alone. Anti-American sentiment is deeply rooted in the British Left; and the fear that Tony Blair was acting as George Bush's 'poodle' was far more widespread in the UK than that. The two together then ate away at popular support for Blair and his war as the evidence mounted that there would be no quick withdrawal of US and UK troops from a 'liberated' Iraq. So that, for example, when Tony Blair was warmly applauded by members of Congress as he addressed them in July 2003, the very applause (and the Congressional gold medal) that he received actually eroded his political standing at home. The tension was visible in the words he chose to deliver there, and in the way in which he called 'history' to his defence. For, having thanked Congress for applause to which he was unaccustomed at home, he said this:

> The risk is that terrorism and states developing weapons of mass destruction come together. When people say that risk is fanciful, I say . . . [i]f we are wrong, we will have destroyed a threat that, at its least is responsible for inhuman carnage and suffering. That is something that I am confident history will forgive. But if our critics are wrong, if we are right as I believe with every fiber of instinct and conviction I have that we are, then we will have hesitated in the face of this menace when we should have given leadership. That is something history will not forgive.[11]

How different in tone and content was this *cri de coeur* from the self-confidence with which the same Tony Blair had faced his critics as they marched in their hundreds of thousands against the impending war in the previous February! Blair in February had not posed the choice in terms of being possibly right or possibly wrong. In February, he had been full of certainties: that Saddam Hussein had weapons of mass destruction and posed a real and immediate danger to his neighbours and to the world. Blair in February had not even privileged the moral case against Saddam Hussein. Far from it: in February, he had been explicit that it was the presence in Iraq of hidden weapons of mass destruction and of potential links to terrorism that could take UK troops into battle there. An earlier Labour Prime Minister, Harold Wilson, had once famously said that a week was a long time in politics. By July 2003, Tony Blair had certainly learned that three months was longer still.

Thus far, the major domestic legacy of the invasion of Iraq by US and UK forces in March 2003 has been a widespread and growing erosion of trust in the honesty and capacity of the politicians who triggered it. This lack of trust has been particularly significant for the Government in London, elected as it was (in both 1997 and 2001) amid a widespread expectation that it would bring a new and higher morality to UK politics. The Iraq war has seriously tarnished the public reputation of New Labour's prime minister. It has undermined political support in the country for the New Labour Government he leads; and it has raised serious questions about the appropriateness of a UK foreign policy that is tied so closely to that of the United States. As Tony Blair's popularity has grown in America and declined at home, critical questions remain unanswered in both countries. *Why did the USA go to war? Why did the UK choose to join the coalition of the willing? Were the USA and the UK right to go to war, or should they have listened to their critics? And are there better – more ethical and more effective – ways of meeting the real security threat and demands for humanitarian intervention that are so prevalent a feature of our post-9/11 world?* These are now the central questions of British politics in the wake of the war's successful military outcome; and inflected in a different way, and directed to George Bush, they are also likely to be the central questions of the presidential campaign of 2004. Because they are, they are also *the* questions which this book intends thoroughly and systematically to explore.

PART I

HOW THE WAR HAPPENED

New Labour: A Leading
Force for Good in the World?

When Tony Blair addressed the US Congress in July 2003 – he was only the fourth UK Prime Minister to be given that honour – he ended his speech with an impassioned declaration of UK support for the United States' post-Cold War global role in the fight against what he called 'the new and deadly virus . . . of terrorism'. 'The spread of freedom', he told Congress, 'is the best security for the free. It is our last line of defence and our first line of attack.' It is not imperialism. 'Ours are not western values. They are the universal values of the human spirit', the ones that, whenever 'ordinary people are given the chance to choose', they take. 'As Britain knows', he said:

> all predominant power seems for a time invincible, but in fact it is transient. The question is: what do you leave behind? What you can bequeath to this anxious world is the light of liberty. This is what the struggle against terrorist groups of states is about. . . . I know it's hard on America. And in some small corner of this vast country . . . there's a guy getting on with his life, perfectly happily, minding his own business, saying . . . why me? Why us? Why America? And the only answer is: because destiny put you in this place in history, in this moment in time and the task is yours to do. And our job, my nation . . . our job is to be there with you. You are not going to be alone. We'll be with you in this fight for liberty.[1]

That Tony Blair was the fourth UK Prime Minister to give Congress his version of this particular speech underscores one of the key elements in the story that we are now to unfold: the long-established presence in UK foreign policy-making circles of an enthusiasm for a 'special relationship' with the USA – what in the language of the trade is referred to as 'Atlanticism'. That Blair was in Washington to make his version of the speech in the wake of the overthrow of Saddam Hussein then underscores the other key element in the story we will tell: the centrality of Iraq to that relationship in the wake of the first Gulf War. New Labour did not create the special relationship. It inherited it. Nor did it put joint action in Iraq on the agenda of that relationship. That too it inherited from its Conservative predecessors. UK jets policed the 'no-fly' zones over northern and southern Iraq long before New Labour came to power, and continued to do so under New Labour foreign secretaries until the overthrow of Saddam Hussein made their task unnecessary. What New Labour added to the relationship and policy it inherited were new ways of understanding the tasks and potential of the special Atlantic relationship, and a particular view of how regimes like those in Baghdad ought properly to be dealt with by the international community. New Labour added, that is, 'a third way' gloss to the foreign policy it inherited; and it was the fusion of that inheritance and that gloss that eventually took UK troops into Basra.

Iraq and the Rise of New Labour

New Labour came to power in 1997, as we will document in a moment, determined to transform UK foreign policy, and was led in that part of its mission (as it would be throughout its first term in office) by the man most associated with that foreign policy transformation: Robin Cook. Both the transformation and the man came to prominence before 1997 in no small measure because of Iraq: or, more precisely, because of the political fall-out from the decision of the Thatcher Government secretly to tolerate the re-arming of Saddam Hussein. Robin Cook came to the Foreign Office, that is, via the Scott Inquiry.

The Scott Inquiry was set in motion by the collapse of the trial of three executives of a machine-tool company, Matrix-Churchill, who had been accused of breaking the arms embargo against Iraq in the late 1980s by exporting machine-making parts that were used for arms production. At their trial in 1992, Alan Clark, a former trade minister, revealed that the Conservative Government under Margaret Thatcher had known about the equipment being exported and had secretly relaxed the rules regarding exports to Iraq. That revelation obliged Margaret Thatcher's successor as Prime Minister, John Major, to set up a public inquiry, headed by Sir Richard Scott. Scott reported in 1996, in a five-volume political bombshell that, according to Cook, revealed 'the price that Britain pays for a culture of secrecy in government'.[2] Cook and the Labour Party had a field day on Iraq at the Conservatives' expense in the wake of the Scott Report. They charged that government ministers had changed the guidelines on defence sales to Saddam Hussein and then repeatedly refused to admit that they had done so, either to Parliament or to the courts, because of the public outrage that this information would have caused. They charged that the intelligence information that the machine tools from Matrix Churchill went into the Iraqi arms programme was, in Sir Richard's words, 'so strong' that for ministers to maintain that they were possibly for civilian use was 'the equivalent to the . . . use of a blind eye'. Cook was incandescent that nobody in the Government was prepared to accept responsibility for the errors that had been highlighted in the report, and resign. How, he asked, was the House of Commons to be expected to 'accept a report which, over five volumes, demonstrates how this Government misjudged Saddam Hussein, misled Members of Parliament and misdirected the prosecution [at the Matrix-Churchill trial], then tell us that no one in the Government will accept responsibility for getting it wrong?'[3]

For Robin Cook and his New Labour colleagues, the arms-to-Iraq scandal and the subsequent Scott Inquiry demonstrated British foreign policy-making and implementation at its worst. The Conservative Government had placed an arms embargo on Iran and Iraq during the war between these countries, and had publicly maintained a position of neutrality towards them both. Secretly, however, it had allowed the export of defence-related equipment to Iraq, thus breaching its own policies on arms exports and on neutrality – and then denied it. New Labour would have none of that. By February 1997 Cook was proposing tighter guidelines for arms exports, including stricter monitoring of end-use certificates, and an annual report of arms sales, giving details of licences granted and refused, which could then be examined by the Commons Select Committees on foreign affairs, defence, and trade and industry. And by May 1997, going to the country with a manifesto that would return it to power in a parliamentary landslide, the entire New Labour leadership was proposing a completely new approach to foreign policy.

This new approach to foreign affairs involved two dimensions, each of which was to play a key part in the subsequent Blairite enthusiasm for war with Iraq. First, Labour in power was to be *more internationalist* than its Conservative predecessors, embracing the interdependence of the modern world, working towards multilateral rather than unilateral solutions to international problems and playing a leading role in Europe. Second, Labour was to have a *more*

<u>*principled*</u> <u>foreign</u> <u>policy</u> <u>than</u> <u>its</u> <u>Conservative</u> <u>predecessors</u>: one that would 'restore Britain's pride and influence as a leading force for good in the world'. In particular, Labour wanted 'Britain to be respected . . . for the integrity with which it conducts its foreign relations', not least by making the 'protection and promotion of human rights a central part of our foreign policy'; working for the creation of a permanent criminal court to investigate genocide, war crimes and crimes against humanity; and accepting that we have a 'moral responsibility to help combat global poverty'.[4]

Rethinking Foreign Policy

Globalization and internationalism

Internationalism, broadly defined, is the desire to transcend national boundaries in order to find solutions to international issues. Robin Cook is and always has been such an internationalist, believing in the need for a strong international community to preserve the peace between nations. Throughout his tenure as Foreign Secretary, this commitment to internationalism could be seen in his willingness to take a multilateral rather than a purely state-centric approach to issues, and in his enthusiasm for international institutions. Cook strongly supported the establishment of an International Criminal Court, the International War Crimes Tribunal on the former Yugoslavia, and the incorporation of the European Convention on Human Rights into UK law. At the 1997 Labour conference he proudly proclaimed that the new Government was now leading negotiations on climate change and the environment, and leading the fight against world poverty.[5] He upgraded the emphasis that the Foreign Office put on cooperative security issues such as international crime, refugees and migration, the proliferation of small arms, and the protection of children in conflict situations. And he shared with Tony Blair the recognition that although 'non-interference has long been considered an important principle of international order', in the new international order, 'the principle of non-interference must be qualified in important respects. Acts of genocide' as Tony Blair told the Economic Club of Chicago in the midst of the Kosovo crisis, 'can never be a purely internal matter.'[6] That shared recognition would take both men, as we will see, into the Kosovo campaign together. It would not, however, later take them together into Iraq.

Armed with this commitment to internationalism, the New Labour Government in its first term saw no tension between its enthusiasm for a deepening of the European Community and the maintenance of a special relationship with the United States. In practice, much of Robin's Cook's workload during Labour's first term was European-focused, while the Washington end of the business was largely fronted by Tony Blair; and neither man publicly conceded that in any basic sense Britain had to choose between Europe and the USA. On the contrary, both insisted that the UK could and should be strong in both arenas. Cook, for example, argued at a 'Britain in Europe' event that 'our political strength is greatly enhanced by playing a leading role in Europe' and that 'it is folly to pretend that Britain has an alternative destiny outside Europe'; but he also argued that 'the paradox that anti-Europeans fail to acknowledge is that far from undermining our special relationship with the United States, our membership of the European Union is increasingly important to the success of that relationship'.[7] This was a theme that Blair also emphasized on numerous occasions. 'We have deluded ourselves for too long', he told the Associated Press, 'with the false choice between the US and Europe.'[8] 'The stronger we are in Europe, the stronger our American relationship.'[9] In fact, both Cook and Blair regularly talked of Britain as 'a natural bridge between our partners in Europe and friends in North America';[10] and the party's 2001 election manifesto reiterated that view, claiming that 'if Britain is stronger in Europe, it will be stronger in the rest of the world. We reject the view of those who say we must choose between Europe and the USA.'[11]

The ease with which New Labour squared the circle of internationalism, European unity and the Anglo-American relationship during its first term in office was enhanced by the closeness of its thinking to that of the Clinton Administration, and by the strong personal relationship that quickly built up between President Clinton and Tony Blair. Both Blair and Clinton wanted to change the world, to reorder it and to spread prosperity, democracy and freedom; and both men wanted this to be done through peaceful means, through collaboration and multilateralism, rather than through confrontation. The two men had a shared perspective on the importance of globalization as a gradual force for harmonizing state interests, and for triggering economic and political reform in countries that were closed off from the rest of the world. Both, that is, shared a 'third way' vision of the link between economic globalization and political democratization;[12] and both men worked closely together on the issue of Iraq.

By the time New Labour came to power in 1997 the Saddam Hussein regime in Baghdad had already survived seven years of, on the most generous of interpretations, only the most minimalist cooperation with the UN inspectorate. So minimal indeed did the Iraqi cooperation become that, after a series of unresolved stand-offs from October 1997, the inspectorate was actually withdrawn from Iraq in December 1998. To that pattern of Iraqi non-compliance and the eventual withdrawal of the inspectors, political circles in the United States then made two broad responses, in the second of which at least the New Labour Government was a willing partner. Late in 1998 Congress passed, and the President signed, the Iraq Liberation Act, which formally committed the USA to the goal of regime change in Baghdad. Much to the irritation of more conservative forces in and around the US foreign-policy establishment, however, this was not a commitment on which the Clinton Administration was pre-pared to do more than fund the Iraqi opposition abroad. It was certainly not prepared to undertake the extensive military action against the Iraqi regime advocated by, among others, Paul Wolfowitz. Instead, and then only in response to the withdrawal of the UN inspectors from Baghdad in December, a beleaguered President Clinton eventually authorized four days of air strikes against Baghdad (Operation Desert Fox) and then a more prolonged intensification of air strikes in the no-fly zones created in the wake of the first Gulf War. These might not have satisfied the signatories to the now widely cited open letter to the President calling for the Administration to make the removal of Saddam Hussein from power 'the aim of Amer-ican foreign policy',[13] but they were substantial air strikes nonethe-less. According to CNN, during 1999 alone, 'US and British war planes bombed Iraq on 138 separate days, attacking more than 450 targets and dropping more than 1,800 bombs';[14] and that bombing continued in 2000 and 2001.

These US military moves against Iraq, and earlier US strikes against 'terrorist targets' in Sudan and Afghanistan, were undertaken with full UK support, and, indeed, attracted to themselves the kind of Blair rhetoric with which the world would become only too familiar in 2003. In the midst of one of the stand-offs between the Iraqis and the UN inspectors, in February 1998, the newly installed UK Prime Minister said this when first visiting the White House:

> We have stood together before in the face of tyranny. Today, in the face of Saddam Hussein, we must stand together once again. We want a diplomatic solution to this crisis. But the success or failure of the diplomacy rests on Saddam. If he fails to respond, then he knows that the threat of force is there, and it is real.[15]

Not surprisingly, therefore, and as Mark Wickham-Jones re-ported later, 'Blair endorsed raids against alleged terrorists ... in

August 1998' and 'he was quick to support and participate in US military initiatives against Iraq in December 1998 when Saddam Hussein refused to comply with weapons inspections.' Significantly, in the light of the events of 2003, 'on both occasions the United Kingdom acted out of step with some of its European partners'.[16] Significantly too, given what was to unfold in 2003, in 1998 Blair gave the USA this support with the full backing of Robin Cook. The man who would personify the political opposition in the UK to the war with Iraq five years later was in 1998, as UK Foreign Secretary, one of the strongest advocates of limited military moves against the Hussein regime.

Robin Cook's capacity to advocate in 1998 what he could not swallow in 2003 turned critically on the differences in policy objectives between the two periods. In 1998/9, the aim of policy was containment and long-term internally generated regime change: it was not, as in 2003, externally imposed regime change. In 1998 Tony Blair was clear on this distinction, and so too was Madeleine Albright, Colin Powell's predecessor as US Secretary of State. 'Is it a specific objective to remove Saddam Hussein?' Tony Blair asked rhetorically, in announcing UK military participation in Operation Desert Fox. 'The answer is it cannot be', even though 'no one would be better pleased if his evil regime disappeared as a direct or indirect result of our action.'[17] When asked what the USA would do if Saddam Hussein persisted in non-compliance with UN resolutions, Madeleine Albright said this:

> I think that we still continue to have the possibilities that we've had before of taking unilateral or multilateral action if we need to. But I think we should – I can't say that we have accomplished everything we've wanted with Iraq, but we, I think, are on the right tracks in keeping them, as I've said, in the box.[18]

No wonder then, that, when questioned later, Robin Cook was well able to justify his different policy stances in 1998 and 2003. 'The case being made four years ago', he told the Foreign Affairs Committee of the House of Commons in June 2003,

> was a very different case. I was not arguing in 1998, none of us were, that Saddam represented an urgent and compelling threat that required preemptive action, which is what was taken in 2003. We carried out a limited number of bombing runs in order to destroy what we believed was the remaining chemical and biological capacity, but we did not attempt to invade the country.[19]

An ethical dimension to foreign policy

In making the case for internationalism in the new global order, both Robin Cook and Tony Blair regularly emphasized that domestic and foreign policy were parts of a whole, and sought to break down the traditional distinction between domestic and foreign affairs. 'We can no longer separate', Tony Blair said, 'what we want to achieve *within* our borders from what we face *across* our borders.'[20] Cook concurred:

> We live in a modern world in which nation states are interdependent. In that modern world foreign policy is not divorced from domestic policy but a central part of any political programme. In order to achieve our goals for the people of Britain we need a foreign strategy that supports the same goals.[21]

Cook, situated as he was on the left of the party, was keen to rethink foreign policy, and for there to be a genuine left-of-centre approach to foreign affairs. That was why he supported the creation of a new left-of-centre think-tank, the Foreign Policy Centre, to 'think the unthinkable' and come up with an innovative approach to foreign policy; that was why he opened up the Foreign Office, holding open days for schools and colleges for the first time in that institution's history; and that was why, in launching his 'mission statement' immediately on taking office in May 1997, he committed New Labour to the implementation of an 'ethical dimension' in its foreign policies. The New Labour Government, he told the assembled journalists, was going to implement a new kind of foreign policy: one with human rights at its heart, and one which 'recognized that the national interest cannot be defined only by narrow *realpolitik*'. The aim, he said, was 'to make Britain once again a force for good in the world'.

> Britain has a national interest in the promotion of our values and confidence in our identity. That is why the fourth goal of our foreign policy is to secure the respect of other nations for Britain's contribution to keeping the peace of the world and promoting democracy around the world. The Labour Government does not accept that political values can be left behind when we check in our passports to travel on diplomatic business. Our foreign policy must have an ethical dimension and must support the demands of other peoples for the democratic rights on which we insist for ourselves. The Labour Government will put human rights at the heart of our foreign policy.[22]

In the event, that proved rather more difficult to do than to say; to such an extent, indeed, that in the autumn of 1998 even the formal commitment to the addition of an ethical dimension to foreign policy was quietly abandoned. It is not of course that the Labour Government has abandoned questions of morality in foreign policy entirely: far from it.

> It is taken for granted that the United Kingdom should not abuse human rights, prohibit economic development or engage in brutal military interventions. Such actions would be without any doubt unethical. Indeed for New Labour the ethical problem is the second-order one of how far the United Kingdom should be responsible for preventing the abuse of human rights carried out by other states or promoting their economic development. The Third Way is premised on the assumption that it is necessary to carve out a route between the extremes of indifference to the plight of others and a moral crusade to put the wrongs of the world to right.[23]

For that reason, this Government did (and does) remain unusually committed, at its most senior levels, to a set of global policies that are ethically progressive. John Prescott, as Deputy Prime Minister, played a key role in the drawing up of the 1998 Kyoto Protocol on climate change. Tony Blair has pushed hard in a whole series of global forums for a northern strategy to alleviate southern poverty; and Gordon Brown, the Chancellor of the Exchequer, was (and remains) a leading voice in the international attempts to alleviate the burden of external debt on some of the globe's poorest economies. Moreover, Robin Cook did have a number of early policy successes that fitted in with his ethical commitment. In May 1997, he announced that the UK would ban the import, export, transfer and manufacture of all forms of anti-personnel landmines, well ahead of the Ottawa conference that made this commitment more universal. Britain hosted the international conference on Nazi gold in December 1997, at which Robin Cook gave a key speech; and Britain, unlike the USA, backed the establishment of an International Criminal Court with powers to order the arrest, trial and punishment of war criminals charged with serious human rights abuses. However, from the very beginning there was a persistent tension between the Foreign Office and Number 10 over the degree to which ethical concerns should and could override the UK's commercial interests abroad. Robin Cook was also criticized for his policy of engagement towards Russia and China, where the New Labour Government invested extensive political capital into strong bilateral relations, and was accused of failing to raise the issue of human rights more strongly. In the case of China, Cook pursued a new policy of 'quiet diplomacy', and in 1998 ended the practice of signing the annual resolution of the UN Commission on Human

Rights condemning China's record on this issue. None of this sat easily with the claim that New Labour's foreign policy was built on strong ethical foundations.

However, the issue that came to be the most closely associated with the ethical dimension of New Labour's foreign policy under Cook was not that of trade with China per se, but that of the export of arms by UK-based companies to countries with a poor record on human rights, including China. This was a key issue for Cook himself, not least because of his stance on such sales to Iraq under the previous Conservative administrations; and indeed, as he had promised then, once in office he did issue new and tougher criteria on the issuing of arms export licences, and did announce that Britain would work for the introduction of a European code of conduct for arms exports. But in practice the release of licences slowed hardly at all; and the new criteria were not applied retrospectively – so allowing the Indonesian regime to acquire already ordered Hawk aircraft, armoured vehicles and water cannon within months of Cook taking office. An early day motion condemning that decision was signed by 136 Labour MPs, who then saw weapons still being exported to other regimes with questionable human rights records, including Colombia, Saudi Arabia, Sri Lanka, Zimbabwe, Turkey and China itself. In fact, it appears that in this area of policy at least, the Foreign and Commonwealth Office (FCO) lost out to the Department of Trade and Industry, and that employment and trade considerations overrode ethical ones.[24] New Labour had an ethical dimension to its foreign policy under Robin Cook: but ethical considerations rarely if ever drove policy in its entirety.

Nowhere was that more evident than in the case of 'arms to Africa' and in particular 'arms to Sierra Leone'. The Sierra Leone case is worth a moment of our time here, as a forerunner to the issues which would beset New Labour later on Iraq: for Sierra Leone was the subject of UN Security Council Resolution (UNSCR) 1132. What happened was this. In 1998, the democratically elected leader of Sierra Leone, President Kabbah, was overthrown by a military coup. Although a number of international organizations, including the United Nations, argued that Kabbah should be returned to power, the international community as a whole was slow to provide resources in support of the restoration of the President. Indeed, both the United States and the EU saw Sierra Leone as essentially an area of British interest; and the FCO went along with that view. So it was the UK that took the lead in mustering international support for Kabbah, maintaining his government in exile and encouraging forces loyal to him. London also funded and equipped a radio station in Sierra Leone in a bid to encourage the forces loyal to the President. However, the British position was complicated by the Labour Government's refusal to provide support to the regional body, the Economic Community of West African States Monitoring Group (ECOMOG), as long as General Sani Abacha, the Nigerian dictator, remained Chairman of the organization. At the 1995 Commonwealth Conference Britain had played a leading role in passing strong condemnation of Abacha's human rights violations within Nigeria. The Foreign Office had insisted on a total ban on assistance to Nigeria. The UN Security Council had invoked sanctions, so by 1998 Britain was actually operating an arms embargo on seventeen countries, including Sierra Leone.

In consequence, the Government, and more specifically Robin Cook and the FCO, were heavily embarrassed by revelations that a British company, Sandline International, had been acting as military consultants in a bid to provide weapons and advisers in support of President Kabbah – weapons and advisers that had eventually aided his return to power. They were even more embarrassed by press allegations that the Foreign Office had known and approved of Sandline's activities. In the event, Robin Cook and his ministers were subsequently exonerated of any attempt to breach the arms embargo,[25] and UK troops did briefly enter Sierra Leone as peacekeepers; but the whole incident served to underscore the degree to which New Labour in power found it difficult to break decisively from well-established patterns of foreign policy – patterns that were not simply Atlanticist but at times of dubious ethical standing as well.

The Kosovo Conflict: A New 'Warlike Humanitarianism'

By far the most important UK foreign policy initiative that laid the grounds for UK involvement in the Iraqi conflict came in Kosovo. Here too, as in Iraq later, public and political opinion in the UK was divided over whether intervention was the right thing to do, morally, politically and strategically; and here too, Tony Blair spoke strongly for those advocating intervention. Unlike the later intervention in Iraq, however, so also did Robin Cook. Both the supporters and the critics of the invasion of Iraq have drawn comfort and inspiration from how the Kosovo crisis was managed; and because they have, the differences between the two crises are of immense importance here.

Robin Cook's interest in Kosovo reflected his earlier concerns over Bosnia. In his 1995 speech to the Labour Party conference, Cook had argued that homeland security included the international defence of Britain's values, and that those values were under attack in Bosnia.

'For the first time since the defeat of fascism', he contended, 'European states are being carved out behind borders drawn up by ethnic cleansing.'[26] Thus, for Cook, when conflict flared up in Kosovo in 1997, it became vital that the international community act to prevent a repetition of what he saw as its failure in Bosnia; and that Britain should play a leading role there, both as a member of the six-nation contact group and (as it happened) through its temporary occupancy of the presidency of the EU. The key events in the Kosovo saga were as follows. In March 1998 Cook hosted an emergency meeting of the Contact Group, which denounced the use of force by both the Serb military and the Kosovo Liberation Army, and called for an arms embargo. This was then passed by the United Nation Security Council as Resolution 1160.[27] However, during the summer of 1998 Cook and Blair resisted German calls for immediate military intervention.[28] Instead, Cook co-chaired talks at Rambouillet with the French Foreign Minister. NATO's military operation then began in March 1999, but only after US diplomat Richard Holbrooke had declared that the final attempt to get Milošević to sign the Rambouillet peace agreement had failed. The UK initially opposed the use of ground troops within that military operation, claiming that air strikes alone would achieve their objective; but by the end of the crisis, the UK had emerged as the strongest voice within the NATO alliance for the deployment of ground troops. Only Milošević's reluctant acquiescence under Russian pressure prevented New Labour's commitment to a ground war in 1999 from being put to the test.

In the case of Kosovo therefore, the Labour Government in the end took a far more interventionist and robust approach to the internal affairs of the former Federal Republic of Yugoslavia than their Conservative predecessors had earlier done in Bosnia. For Tony Blair in 1998 and 1999, intervention was the morally right thing to do. It reflected Britain's new approach to foreign and security policy, and the desire that Britain act as a force for good in the world. Robin Cook was entirely with him on this, and even rallied left-wing support by making several comparisons of the Kosovo situation to the Spanish Civil War and the failure of the international community to support the Spanish people in their fight against fascism, proclaiming that:

> I am absolutely robust that we are right to be fighting this evil. There is no conflict between the traditional values of the left and being against this. What we are witnessing is the resurgence of fascism in Europe. . . . We have not seen trains used to take men, women and children from their homes since the days of Hitler and Stalin. I do not think that anyone on the left should have any reservations about fighting this evil.[29]

Here then was a new element in foreign policy. Military intervention by UK forces in Kosovo represented a new approach in London, confirmed with considerably less fanfare by the deployment of troops to Sierra Leone in 2000 to quell the political violence and to support UN initiatives. Under Robin Cook, the UK was prepared to countenance intervention by forces for humanitarian reasons if that intervention was mandated by international organizations (in the Kosovo case, by NATO) and if the regime under attack represented a stark challenge to basic human rights. The new approach did not privilege the territorial sovereignty of nation-states – the principle that alone had guided the first Gulf War. Instead, it insisted that states forfeited their right to territorial sovereignty when they abused their own people. The new approach legitimated what we might call 'warlike humanitarianism' as the foreign policy of the centre-left. It also, as it happened, opened the door to the New Labour Government's willingness in 2003 to go to war in Iraq, in spite of the absence of any direct and immediate military threat from Iraq to the UK itself. It did not make that willingness inevitable – Robin Cook, after all, would be Tony Blair's chief critic in 2003. But it certainly opened the door to it. The Kosovo conflict was significant for British foreign policy in that it was the first time in NATO's history that the alliance had undertaken a sustained military campaign, and one aimed at preventing a humanitarian tragedy rather than a military threat to a member state. It was also significant for Tony Blair in that it was the most dramatic crisis to which he had to respond during his first premiership. It not only highlighted his new, more internationalist and interventionist approach to foreign policy, but also amplified his increasingly leading role in British foreign policy. The Kosovo crisis demonstrated to the bulk of the New Labour leadership that the use of force and intervention was sometimes the 'right' thing to do for humanitarian reasons; and it gave Tony Blair his first training in global military leadership. What 9/11 then added, as we will now see, was an extra set of reasons for the Blairite wing of New Labour to combine military with peaceful means in its attempt to be a force for good in the world.

The American Call to Arms

United States administrations rarely hit the ground running, and the new Bush Administration definitely did not do so. It had begun its term uncertain in its domestic policy because of the legitimacy gap triggered by its long court battle to capture Florida's electoral college vote; and it had begun its term uncertain in its foreign policy because of deep divisions of approach at its very highest levels. The transition team headed by Vice-President-elect Cheney staffed the State Department under Colin Powell with people who were broadly multilateralist in their understandings of US foreign policy needs, but it also placed in senior positions in the Pentagon men who had served Republican Administrations before, and who had their own as yet unfinished and more unilateralist policy agenda. In the event, and as if in negative response to the global activism of the Clinton Administration, the second Bush presidency settled in its first year into what began to look like a new isolationism. Its Secretary of State still flew around the world, but its President did not. He talked a new language that explicitly put immediate domestic US interests first, pulled the United States out of the Kyoto Accords, and washed his hands of direct personal intervention in the ongoing search for peace in the Middle East.

Responding to 9/11

The attack on the World Trade Center and the Pentagon on 11 September 2001 changed all that. For the American people, as well as for its President, the events of 9/11 represented a second Pearl Harbor;

and, like the attack on Pearl Harbor, they required and received a sustained and serious US diplomatic and military response. We know now, from the journalism of Bob Woodward among others, that initially the Bush Administration struggled to find that response. But when it did find it, its first moves set its foreign policy in a frame which, once created, was never abandoned. Within 24 hours of the attacks, the Bush Administration had settled into a crucial set of definitions of its new situation. The attacks were defined as acts of war. Their perpetrators were not soldiers or members of an international criminal conspiracy, but terrorists. Defence against them required not simply homeland security, but total victory. That victory meant the physical annihilation of both the terrorists and their structures of support. So the enemies to be annihilated were not simply the terrorists themselves; they were also the regimes that harboured them.

All the major figures in the drama then to unfold are on record during that September as reading the situation in that way. George Bush himself made the key opening statements in a brief radio address to the American people on 15 September and to Congress on 20 September. 'Victory against terrorism', he told a radio audience still reeling from the shock of the attacks themselves, 'will not take place in a single battle, but in a series of decisive actions against terrorist organizations and those who harbor and support them.'[1] 'Our war on terror begins with al-Qaeda', he told a congressional and world audience that included Tony Blair, 'but it does not end there. It will not end until every terrorist group of global reach has been found, stopped and defeated.' Accordingly:

[The US] will direct every resource at our command – every means of diplomacy, every tool of intelligence, every instrument of law enforcement, every financial influence, and every necessary weapon of war – to the disruption and to the defeat of the global terror network. This war will not be like the war against Iraq a decade ago, with a decisive liberation of territory and a swift conclusion. It will not look like the air war above Kosovo two years ago, where no ground troops were used and not a single American was lost in combat. Our response involves far more than instant retaliation and isolated strikes. Americans should not expect one battle, but a lengthy campaign, unlike any other we have ever seen. It may include dramatic strikes, visible on television, and covert operations, secret even in success. We will starve terrorists of funding, turn them one against another, drive them from place to place, until there is no refuge and no rest. And we will pursue nations that provide aid or safe haven to terrorism. Every nation, in every region, now has a decision to take. Either you are with us, or you are with the terrorists. From this day forward, any nation that continues to harbor or support terrorism will be regarded by the United States as a hostile regime.[2]

Powell, Donald Rumsfeld and Wolfowitz all then followed suit. Powell, for example, was quick to tell reporters in the wake of the President's speech, that:

> I was raised a soldier and . . . trained: there is the enemy occupying a piece of ground. We can define it in time, space and other dimensions, and you can assemble forces and go after it. This is different. The enemy is in many places. The enemy is not looking to be found. The enemy is hidden. The enemy is very often right here within our own country. And so you have to design a campaign plan that goes after that kind of enemy, and it isn't always blunt military force, although that is certainly an option. It may well be that the diplomatic efforts, political efforts, legal, financial, other efforts may be just as effective against that kind of an enemy as would military force be.[3]

In putting it in that way, Powell was characteristically cautious about the military option. Privately, other Administration figures were less so; and yet initially Powell's was the official line: that the USA would develop a response that was broad in conception and international support, and in which military action would be only one dimension. This will be, Secretary of Defense Rumsfeld told the *New York Times* on 27 September, 'a new kind of war', one that requires different kinds of coalition, a mixture of methods of attack, a blend of covert and overt actions, even a new vocabulary to describe its purposes and methods. But like all wars, Rumsfeld insisted, it would end with a victor: and in this war, in the Administration's view, victory would mean 'liquidating the terrorist networks and putting them out of business' and 'crippling the ability of terrorist organizations, and the states that sponsor them, to coerce our nation, intimidate our people and disrupt our way of life'.[4] In such a war, as Paul Wolfowitz put it more graphically, 'we are not just going to pick off individuals. We intend to drain the entire swamp'.[5]

The critical initial issue to be settled, of course, was which particular swamp the USA ought to drain first; and on this, and from the outset, the Administration was divided. Majority opinion within the top policy-making circles around the President in the opening months of what he had properly described as being, inevitably, a long and drawn out process, was that the first swamp to be drained was that of Afghanistan – on the not unreasonable grounds that it was the Taliban regime there that allowed al-Qaeda (the network whose members had indeed carried out the attacks of 9/11) to recruit, train and organize on its territory. That was the majority view, and indeed Bush's own: and it was one shared by a whole string of international organizations and their constituent national states. It immediately became the accepted position of the UK Government; it quickly became the accepted position within NATO; and it eventually became the accepted position within the Security Council of the UN. It became so accepted there, in fact, that when US and UK forces moved against the Taliban in November 2001, the coalition of support behind that military action included the armies of sixteen other nations and the intelligence services of at least seventy more.[6] But it was never the unambiguously accepted position within the entirety of the Bush Administration as a whole.

If Bob Woodward's reporting is accurate,[7] Rumsfeld and Wolfowitz wanted the swamp to include Iraq from the very outset. Powell did not, and the matter was initially argued out in a key policy debate at Camp David on the first weekend after the World Trade Center attacks. The way Woodward tells it:

> [The Pentagon] had been working for months on developing a military option for Iraq [under the guidance of what he calls] an outspoken group of national security conservatives in Washington, many of them veterans of the Reagan and senior Bush administrations. These were men who believed that there was no greater menace in the world than Iraqi President Saddam Hussein, and they argued that if the president was serious about going after those who harbor terrorists, he had to put Hussein at the top of that list.[8]

Powell, by contrast, wanted the focus kept on al-Qaeda and on Afghanistan, because that was the known linkage and that was the campaign around which the broadest coalition of support could be mobilized. Woodward reports him as keen to get Rumsfeld and Wolfowitz 'back in the box'.[9] Certainly, when Wolfowitz went public in September with his view that the USA was now in the business of 'ending regimes that sponsor terrorism', Powell declined to line up with him, preferring instead simply to respond in the following manner when asked:

> QUESTION Are we really after ending regimes, or are we simply going to try to change their behavior?

> SECRETARY POWELL We are after ending terrorism. And if there are states and regimes, nations, that support terrorism, we hope to persuade them that it is in their interests to stop doing that. But I think ending terrorism is where I would like to leave it, and let Mr Wolfowitz speak for himself.[10]

In the light of what was eventually to transpire, however, what is striking about the first phase of the US response to the events of 9/11 is that Wolfowitz's preoccupation with Iraq did not prevail. The US Administration did remain primarily focused on Afghanistan, and on Afghanistan alone. Yet the issue of Iraq never entirely went away. It simply spent the last months of 2001 on the back burner – mentioned, deflected, put on hold – understood as an issue to be addressed later, then ideally to be handled (at least in the State Department's view) in the same broad coalitional manner as Afghanistan. As early as 13 September 2001, Powell was asked if 'he could talk about links between Iraq and Osama bin Laden?' and he said he could and would not;[11] and when asked again in October, he similarly refused to be drawn. 'Is Iraq next?' the reporter wanted to know. 'No', Powell said; 'the President decided this a month ago, and we've been following the President's guidance ever since.' When asked what that decision had been, Powell insisted that it was 'that in this campaign, we are focusing in the first instance on al-Qaeda as it exists throughout the world, especially its headquarters in Afghanistan ... but also at the same time that it is terrorism around the world that we are after.'[12]

Significantly, however, when pushed on the matter yet again as the military campaign in Afghanistan moved towards its successful conclusion, Powell continued to hold the line, but by then only in a way that showed that the line was clearly beginning to slip. This was Powell, quizzed in December 2001:

> QUESTION Mr Secretary, everyone in the world ... wonders if Iraq will be the next on the line in [the] war against terrorism.

> SECRETARY POWELL The President has indicated for a long time that we are concerned about Iraq, that it tries to develop weapons of mass destruction. We're doing everything we can to keep it from getting such weapons. Such weapons are dangerous to the region as well as to the world. We also know that Iraq has been a sponsor of terrorism over the years, and that continues to be a concern of ours. But the President has made no decisions with respect to what the next phase of our campaign against terrorism might be ... nor has he received any recommendations yet from his advisors as to what we might do next.[13]

Though formally true, that last claim was by then disingenuous. For as the military campaign in Afghanistan moved to its climax in December, so too did the efforts of the hawks in the Administration to shape any new military action to come. Deputy Secretary of Defense

Wolfowitz had already told both the House and Senate armed forces committees in October that the United States now needed a new kind of military, one that had learned the lessons of 9/11. Among those lessons, Wolfowitz then insisted, was that the USA's 'new adversaries may be, in some cases, more dangerous than those . . . faced in the past', because 'they were less likely to be discouraged by traditional deterrence' and 'because their decision making is not subject to the same constraints' as that of earlier adversaries. Osama bin Laden was offered by the Deputy Secretary as one of three examples of such new adversaries. Significantly, the other two were Saddam Hussein and the North Korean leader Kim Jong Il.[14]

Likewise, when addressing NATO ministers in Brussels in December, Donald Rumsfeld chose to emphasize that, in the view of the US Administration, 'the war was far from over'. For, as he put it:

> Afghanistan is not the only country where terrorists operate, and al-Qaeda is not the only terrorist network that threatens us. Terrorist networks function in dozens of countries, often with the support of terrorist regimes. [The President has said that] every nation knows that we cannot accept – and will not accept – states that harbor, finance, train or equip the agents of terror. Those nations . . . will be regarded as hostile regimes. They have been warned, they're being watched, and they will be held to account.

No names were mentioned by the Secretary of Defense on this particular occasion, but the range of the possible was definitely being ratcheted down. For why else would he tell the NATO ministers that 'it should be of particular concern to all of us that the list of countries which today support global terrorism overlaps significantly with the list of countries that have weaponized chemical and biological agents, and which are seeking nuclear, chemical and biological weapons – and the means to deliver them'.[15] Which countries the Secretary had in mind, he then publicly declined to say; but the world did not have to wait long to find out. It had to wait only until George W. Bush made his State of the Union Address to Congress on 29 January 2002. It only had to wait until then to find Iraq singled out as a member of 'an axis of evil'.

The Targeting of Iraq

By the time that the State of the Union address was given, the focus of the Bush Administration's war on terrorism was shifting away from Afghanistan towards what the President that evening called 'governments . . . timid in the face of terror' and 'regimes that sponsor terror'. It was shifting to three in particular. The words were important:

> Some of these regimes have been pretty quiet since September the 11th. But we know their true nature. North Korea is a regime arming with missiles and weapons of mass destruction, while starving its citizens. Iran aggressively pursues those weapons and exports terror, while an unelected few repress the Iranian people's hope for freedom.
>
> Iraq continues to flaunt its hostility towards America and to support terror. The Iraqi regime has plotted to develop anthrax, and nerve gas, and nuclear weapons for over a decade. This is a regime that has already used poison gas to murder thousands of its own citizens – leaving the bodies of mothers huddled over their dead children. This is a regime that agreed to international inspections – then kicked out the inspectors. This is a regime that has something to hide from the civilized world.
>
> States like these, and their terrorist allies, constitute an axis of evil, arming to threaten the peace of the world. By seeking weapons of mass destruction, these regimes pose a grave and growing danger. They could provide these arms to terrorists, giving them the means to match their hatred. They could attack our allies or attempt to blackmail the United States. In any of these cases, the price of indifference would be catastrophic.[16]

This 'price of indifference' formulation was in truth the world's first exposure to what later would be widely recognized as 'the Bush doctrine'. It signified an emerging willingness on the part of the US Government to move pre-emptively, and if necessary alone, against governments that in its view constituted a threat to US security interests. On its first public showing, the doctrine was given its most multilateralist formulation, but it was given nonetheless:

> We will work closely with our coalition to deny terrorists and their state sponsors the materials, technology and expertise to make and deliver weapons of mass destruction. We will develop and deploy effective missile defenses to protect America and our allies from sudden attack. And all nations should know: America will do what is necessary to ensure our nation's security. We will deliberate, yet time is not on our side. *I will not wait on events, while dangers gather. I will not stand by, as peril grows closer and closer. The United States of America will not permit the world's most dangerous regimes to threaten us with the world's most destructive weapons.* Our war on terror is well begun, but it is only begun. The campaign may not be finished on our watch – yet it must be and it will be waged on our watch.[17]

In the event, however, other items of foreign policy took centre stage during the first half of 2002 as the Administration's policy on Iraq developed largely in private. But nonetheless, that development did occur. Covert operations against Saddam Hussein intensified and secret planning for a possible invasion began. *Time* magazine had the decision to plan for a militarily imposed regime change in Baghdad being made as early as March 2002, a date subsequently (if inadvertently) confirmed by General Tommy Franks in an unscripted exchange with journalists;[18] and the President was, as ever, periodically quizzed by the press on his attitude to an Iraqi regime that he was secretly working to bring down. He was so quizzed, for example, when visited by Tony Blair in Texas in April. He said this:

> The Prime Minister and I of course talked about Iraq. We both recognize the danger of a man who is willing to kill his own people and harboring and developing weapons of mass destruction. This guy, Saddam Hussein, is a leader who gasses his own people, goes after people in his own neighborhood with chemical weapons, he is a man who obviously has something to hide. He told the world he would show us that he would not develop weapons of mass destruction, and yet over the past decade he has refused to do so. And the Prime Minister and I both agree that he needs to prove that he isn't developing weapons of mass destruction. I explained to the Prime Minister that the policy of my government is the removal of Saddam and that all options are on the table. . . . The world would be better off without him . . . and so would the future. You see the worst thing that can happen is to allow this man to abrogate his promise and hook up with the terrorist network and then all of a sudden you have got one of these shadowy terrorist networks that have got an arsenal at their disposal which could create a situation in which nations down the road get blackmailed, and we can't let that happen, we just can't let that happen.
>
> And obviously the Prime Minister is someone who understands this clearly and this is why I appreciate dealing with him on the issue and we have got close consultations going on, we talk about it all the time and he has got very good advice on the subject and I appreciate that.[19]

Given the nature of that advice – that the best way to handle the threat posed by Saddam Hussein was to build a broad coalition of support for any action to be taken – the official Administration answer throughout the spring and summer of 2002, the one the President invariably gave, was always the same. It was that the regime of Saddam Hussein was a problem with which the world would soon need to deal, that the United States was consulting widely with its allies on how best to proceed, and that in the meantime (and this as late as August 2002) he, the President, 'had no timetable for any of our policies as regards to Iraq'.[20] But both behind the scenes and in a series of television interviews and speeches Vice-President Cheney was regularly keeping the issue of Iraq high on the policy agenda, even though in public at least the attention of key figures in the Bush Administration, including that of Cheney himself, was ostensibly focused in the first half of 2002 on other things. It was focused on the ABM treaty, on Israeli-Palestinian violence, on homeland security and on the restructuring of the US military.

Meanwhile, however, the organizing principles of the Bush doctrine were being quietly consolidated and enshrined in policy. In May the early drafts of the National Security Strategy document that would be released in September – leaked to the *Los Angeles Times* – committed the US Government to 'proactive counter proliferation efforts' and promised that, 'as a matter of common sense and self-defense, America will act against . . . emerging threats *before they are fully formed*. . . . To forestall or prevent . . . hostile acts by our adversaries', the document said, 'the United States will, if necessary, act preemptively.'[21] In June, the President went public on that policy to the annual crop of West Point graduates paraded before him. He told them:

> [T]he gravest danger to freedom lies at the perilous crossroads of radicalism and technology. When the spread of chemical and biological and nuclear weapons, along with ballistic missile technology – when that occurs, even weak states and small groups could attain a catastrophic power to strike great nations. Our enemies have declared this very intention, and have been caught seeking these terrible weapons. They want the capability to blackmail us, or to harm us, or to harm our friends – and we will oppose them with all our power. For much of the last century, America's defense relied on the Cold War doctrines of deterrence and containment. In some cases, those strategies still apply. But new threats also require new thinking. Deterrence – the promise of massive retaliation against nations – means nothing against shadowy terrorist networks with no nation or citizens to defend. Containment is not possible when unbalanced dictators with weapons of mass destruction can deliver those weapons on missiles or secretly provide them to terrorist allies.
>
> We cannot defend America and our friends by hoping for the best. We cannot put our faith in the word of tyrants, who solemnly sign non-proliferation treaties, and then systematically break them. If we wait for threats to fully materialize, we will have waited too long. Homeland defense and missile defense are part of stronger security, and they're essential priorities for America. Yet the war on terror will not be won on the defensive. We must take the battle to the enemy, disrupt his plans, and confront the worst threats before they emerge. In the world we have entered, the only path to safety is the path of action. And this nation will act.[22]

It should not be thought, however, that at any time during 2002 the State Department abandoned its attempt to ensure that this action, when it came, would take, as in the case of Afghanistan, a broadly multilateralist form. Far from it: armed with a coalition of more than sixty nations and widespread global sympathy for the United States in the wake of 9/11, Powell would have been remiss if he had not struggled against policies that would dissipate this key foreign policy resource; and anyway Woodward reports him as being in full agreement with Brent Scowcroft in mid-2002 that 'an attack on Iraq could turn the Middle East into a "cauldron and thus destroy the war on terrorism"'.[23] Impatient as the hawks were to go after Iraq, and if need be to go alone, Powell still managed to persuade the President to take the UN route. In August, if Bob Woodward's journalism is again sound, Powell reportedly put the case against unilateral action, emphasizing its adverse effects on Arab opinion, its economic and diplomatic costs and the sheer logistical difficulties involved in its implementation. It is significant, of course, that by August he felt that he had to make the case, so strong were the rumblings at the top level of the Bush team that, in the case of Iraq, the USA should act soon and act alone. But even so, in August at least, Powell appeared to prevail. He won the grudging approval of even Cheney and Rumsfeld that US policy against Iraq should, in the first instance, be orchestrated through the UN. He won agreement that, as had been the case since 1998, the USA would push, as its Iraq policy, for the return of the UN inspectorate to Iraq, and for full Iraqi compliance with existing UN resolutions.[24]

Which is why Vice-President Cheney's 27 August speech then came as such a bombshell, putting as it did a huge question-mark over the credibility of that policy within days of it being apparently settled within the Administration. Addressing the Veterans of Foreign Wars National Convention, Cheney launched a long and detailed criticism of the Iraqi regime, and made clear his own scepticism about the UN's capacity to control its excesses. For the benefit of the veterans, he rehearsed Saddam Hussein's record on both internal brutality and external aggression, and then made an explicit call for 'regime change in Iraq' as the route to better opportunities for general Middle East peace. Labelling Hussein 'a sworn enemy of our country', he charged him with a series of specific things, namely:

- systematically breaking each of the agreements made with the UN in the wake of the 1991 Gulf War;
- actively enhancing his capabilities in the field of chemical and biological agents;

- resuming his efforts to acquire nuclear weapons;
- beginning again to test his missile programme, in spite of its illegality under the UN agreements;
- devising elaborate schemes to obscure all this rearmament;
- frustrating and deceiving the UN inspectors at every stage;
- dispatching a team of assassins to murder former President George H. W. Bush.

'Simply stated,' Cheney said, 'there is no doubt that Saddam Hussein now has weapons of mass destruction' and that 'he is amassing them to use against our friends, against our allies and against us.' Because of that, in Cheney's view, the argument for action to disarm and replace Saddam Hussein was overwhelming, since 'should all his ambitions be realized, the implications would be enormous for the Middle East, for the United States and for the peace of the world'. The implications that the Vice-President then listed were of doomsday proportions: Saddam Hussein 'could then be expected to seek domination of the entire Middle East, take control of a great portion of the world's energy supplies, directly threaten America's friends throughout the region, and subject the United States or any other nation to nuclear blackmail'.

'In the face of such a threat,' Cheney told his audience, 'we must proceed with care, deliberation, and consultation with our allies'; but we should be under no illusion that the return of the UN inspectors would be in any way enough. Again, the words are important:

> Against that background, a person would be right to question any suggestion that we should just get inspectors back into Iraq, and then our worries will be over. Saddam has perfected the game of cheat and retreat, and is very skilled in the art of denial and deception. A return of inspectors would provide no assurance whatsoever of his compliance with UN resolutions. On the contrary, there is a great danger that it would provide false comfort that Saddam was somehow 'back in the box'.[25]

So the Bush Administration went off to the UN sending mixed signals: officially committed to the achievement of new UN resolutions that would strengthen a returned inspectorate – this was President Bush's declared aim before the UN in his address to the Assembly on 12 September – but privately battling over the view that Woodward attributes to Cheney: that even 'to ask for a new resolution would put them back in the soup of the UN process – hopeless, endless and irresolute'.[26] Those divisions were publicly known throughout the long diplomatic offensive that ultimately produced UNSCR 1441: and because they were known, many of the countries signing up to it agreed to a new resolution only on the understanding that it was not a green light for US military intervention in Iraq if the renewed inspections met Iraqi resistance and deception again. The US Administration went to the UN in September seeking a new and tougher resolution on the inspection of Iraqi weapons of mass destruction. It went to the US Congress that same month seeking the power to trigger immediate, and if need be unilateral, military intervention if that inspection process stalled. It got the latter; and because it did, nervousness within the broad coalition that had mobilized against Afghanistan intensified still further.

Multilateralism's Last Stand

The diplomatic initiative launched by Colin Powell, and actively supported by the UK Government, did produce a new UN resolution, and did get the UN inspectors back into Iraq before the end of 2002. Multilateralism had its moment; but it was always a conditional one. Even Colin Powell was clear on that:

QUESTION Mr Secretary, you used the word multilateral views as expressed in the UN Security Council, and after some of your meetings today, some of your counterparts came out and said that they do not support US unilateral action, but would support some kind of multilateral approach to deal with the problem of Iraq. As you talk about multilateral views, do you think that the Bush Administration will take a multilateral approach?

SECRETARY POWELL The President made it clear today that he has every intention of consulting widely . . . with our friends and allies and with the UN. He at the same time made it clear that we preserve all our options to do what we believe is necessary to deal with this problem. I think to pigeonhole it as multilateral or unilateral [is wrong] – what we're trying to do now is to make sure that the world understands the threat as clearly as we believe it should understand this threat, because it is a real one. We cannot allow the international community to be thwarted in this effort to require Iraq to comply.[27]

This, in September, when questions were asked too about the sudden urgency with which the 'world' now had to 'understand the threat'. What had changed? The answer was: 'weapons of mass destruction'. Powell again:

> [T]his regime continues to move in this direction of developing weapons
> of mass destruction. This is not in dispute . . . the intelligence case is
> clear that they have weapons of mass destruction of one kind or another,
> and they are trying to develop more. . . . With a regime such as Iraq . . .
> this is not something you can just turn your head and forget about or
> look away.[28]

Which was why, when George Bush addressed the UN General
Assembly later that same month, he effectively put the international
body on notice: that the USA would go through the UN just so long
as the UN went along with what the US Administration had decided
was in its (and the international community's) best interests. The
USA would work through the UN – this was Powell's victory – but if
the UN failed to act effectively, the USA would act for it – this was
Cheney's: multilateralism in form but unilateralism in substance. 'The
conduct of the regime', Bush told the General Assembly, was 'a threat
to the authority of the United Nations and a threat to peace.' Its acts
of defiance for over a decade now presented the UN with 'a difficult
and defining moment': either to insist that its resolutions be implemented, or to become 'irrelevant'. The President said:

> My nation will work with the UN Security Council to meet our com-
> mon challenge. If Iraq's regime defies us again, the world must move
> deliberately, decisively to hold Iraq to account. We will work with the
> UN Security Council for the necessary resolutions. But the purposes of
> the United States should not be doubted. The Security Council resolu-
> tions will be enforced – the just demands of peace and security will be
> met – or action will be unavoidable.[29]

This was the message that Defense Secretary Rumsfeld then took
to the Hill in the pursuit of congressional authorization for war: that
'Iraq is part of the global war on terror' because 'stopping terrorist
regimes from acquiring weapons of mass destruction is a key objective of that war'. But he took more than the message. He also took
with him to the Hill a healthy dose of Cheney-like scepticism on
whether even a reinforced regime of UN inspectors would be effective in this case. 'The purpose of inspections,' he told the House Armed
Services Committee,

> is to prove that Iraq has disarmed, which would require that Iraq
> would reverse its decade-long policy of pursuing these weapons, and
> that is certainly something that Iraq is unlikely to do. Even the most
> intrusive inspection regime would have difficulty getting at all his weap-
> ons of mass destruction. Many . . . are mobile. They can be hidden

from inspectors no matter how intrusive. He has vast underground networks and facilities, and sophisticated denial and deception techniques. There is a place for inspections. They tend to be effective if the target nation is actually willing to disarm and wants to prove to the world that they're doing so. They tend not to be as effective in uncovering deceptions and violations when the target is determined not to disarm and to try to deceive. And Iraq's record of the past decade shows that they want weapons of mass destruction and are determined to continue to develop them.[30]

Rumsfeld was also unwilling that day to concede in public that, if the new inspection process worked, regime change in Baghdad would be unnecessary. When pressed at length on this point by Representative Tom Allen (Democrat) from Maine, the Secretary of Defense repeatedly hedged. He insisted that such a policy change was so unlikely as to be purely hypothetical, and passed responsibility on this key issue up to the White House and back to the representatives themselves.

ALLEN Assume you get to a place where you're satisfied that, through a combination of Iraqi cooperation and a robust inspections regime, that you get to a place where you're satisfied as an administration that Iraq has effectively dismantled and disarmed its weapons of mass destruction, but Saddam Hussein is still in power, would that . . .

RUMSFELD Well, that's a reach.

ALLEN It's a reach, I know. I know. I grant you this is a hypothetical. But sometimes we get places by asking hypotheticals.

RUMSFELD Sure.

ALLEN If that happens, would that satisfy the Administration's goal?

RUMSFELD The Congress, of course, has adopted a policy for the United States of America of regime change. Are you suggesting that if there was the certainty of disarmament, because of a regime that was so incredibly intrusive that, notwithstanding a regime that was against disarmament you were able to achieve disarmament, would the Congress then want to change the law and back away from regime change . . .

ALLEN . . . my question was not about what Congress might or might not do. I grant you that's hard to determine. My question was really about the Administration and what the Administration's policies would be. There are lots of dictators that we have allowed to continue in operation around the globe. We haven't set a policy of replacing them all. I'm trying to get at where the Administration is with respect to weapons of mass destruction. I grant you it's a reach to assume that there is a change of position of the current Iraqi regime, but if there were, would that be enough?

RUMSFELD That, of course, is a judgment not for the secretary of defense of the United States. It's a judgment for the president and the Congress.[31]

The ducking and weaving brought this frustrated outburst from Representative Lindsey Graham (Republican) of South Carolina:

Why don't we just be honest with people? Everybody in the administration has been telling us that Saddam Hussein has to go . . . no matter what we do with inspections. . . . We just need to level with people, here in this country and in the world: post 9/11, we view Saddam Hussein as a threat to this country, period.

And if that's the case, when we go consult our allies and consult the UN, we should tell them that is our view. I think there's some mixed messages going on here, and I think we need to be very clear with the American public and with our allies.[32]

There were, however, no mixed messages when George Bush addressed the American people from Cincinnati in October, a speech that was watched by millions in the United States as public opinion shifted behind the Administration's call for regime change in Baghdad. Nor were there any mixed messages when Deputy Defense Secretary Wolfowitz addressed the Fletcher conference in Washington a week later. Bush emphasized that 'the threat from Iraq stands alone – because it gathers the most serious dangers of our age in one place'.[33] Wolfowitz put those dangers together:

Because of this connection between states developing weapons of mass destruction and terrorist organizations willing to use them without any compunction and in an undeterrable fashion . . . we cannot continue living safely with a regime [which the President detailed as having] links to international terrorists [and] training al-Qaeda members in bomb-making, poisons and deadly gasses. The President spoke about Iraq's growing fleet of unmanned aerial vehicles that could disburse its arsenal of biological and chemical weapons, and about the ominous fact that Iraq is exploring ways of using these UAVs for missions targeting the United States. And, of course, as the President said . . . sophisticated delivery systems are not required for a chemical or biological attack. All that might be required are a small container and one terrorist or Iraqi intelligence operative to deliver it.[34]

In fact, when Wolfowitz was pressed later on the issue of the evidence underpinning the claims made by Administration figures as they put the case for military action to Congress and the American people, he was characteristically candid about the uncertainties of the data on offer. He said this, in an exchange that went entirely unnoticed at the time:

> There's a lot of ambiguities here, and we're trying to state the facts as we know them and as they develop. And I think the word 'facts' is probably better than 'evidence'. Evidence implies that you're going to get proof, and forget about – I mean, in a court of law, you need proof. In predicting where dangers lie to the United States, you have to make judgments about whether something is 10% likely or 50% likely or 80% likely. . . . So you weigh all these things, and these facts that we have. . . . Facts about a decade of senior-level contact between Iraq and al-Qaeda, facts about Iraq training of al-Qaeda people, including in chemical and biological weapons, and facts about Iraq providing sanctuary for al-Qaeda people, including senior al-Qaeda people, including in Baghdad. Combine that with the fact that the President referred to in his speech, which is not about al-Qaeda but is about Iraq, that we know they're working on unmanned aerial vehicles, the capability of targeting the United States, and you begin to have facts that I think you have to make judgments against. But let me again emphasize the underlying uncertainty of all this.[35]

It was 'facts' such as these, and 'the judgments made on facts' such as these that drove Administration policy both before and after the passing of UNSCR 1441 towards a military confrontation with Saddam Hussein; but it was the 'underlying uncertainty' of many of those facts that left the Administration over time taking that journey largely on its own.

Mobilizing a 'Coalition of the Willing'

UNSCR 1441 passed unanimously on 8 November 2002. It condemned Iraq for its 'material breach' of previous UN resolutions on weaponry, human rights and terrorism, and for the absence of international inspection since December 1998. It demanded 'full and immediate compliance by Iraq without conditions or restrictions with its obligations' under those resolutions, and gave Iraq 'one final opportunity to comply'. Compliance was to take the form of full cooperation with 'an enhanced inspection regime', initially by the production by Iraq within thirty days of a full dossier of its existing stock of relevant weaponry, and cooperation with inspectors on the ground within forty-five days. 'False statements or omissions' in that report 'and failure by Iraq . . . to comply with, and cooperate fully in the implementation of, this resolution' would constitute a 'further material breach of Iraq's obligations'; and such failure, the resolution concluded, would leave Iraq facing *serious consequences* at the hands of the international community as a whole. The precise nature of those consequences was not spelled out in UNSCR 1441, but the resolution did indicate the procedure that their generation would require: namely action by the Security Council in the light of reports back from the inspectors, with their first report due in sixty days.

From the very moment of its passing, UNSCR 1441 was given the very tightest of interpretations by leading figures in the Bush Administration, so tight in fact that the American interpretation twisted the meaning of the resolution in a way that widened the diplomatic breach with the Security Council members who wanted war to be truly a last resort. While the Americans insisted that fabrications or omissions in the declaration made by Iraq were sufficient grounds to constitute an additional material breach and trigger serious consequences, those who opposed the rush to war insisted that 1441 be read as it was written: however unsatisfactory the declaration might be, full cooperation with the enhanced inspection regime would keep the sword of Damocles from falling, if only by a thread. With little trust in either camp, the arguments for war rested on disagreements about 'and' or 'or' in UNSCR 1441, and on the significance and role of the inspectors now gaining extensive access across Iraq. It was not the inspectors' job, Deputy Secretary of Defense Wolfowitz insisted, to scour every inch of Iraq, looking for hidden weapons. It was not their job to play what Powell later called 'rope-a-dope in the desert'.[36] On the contrary, it was the responsibility of the Iraqis to provide 'credible and accurate and complete' information without 'any act of delay or defiance'.[37] It was up to them to prove to the international community that they were disarming. The burden of proof lay on them, not on the international community and its inspectors. The UN was sending in inspectors, not detectives.[38] Iraqi disarmament had to be voluntary and rapid, the President said in Prague; for 'if Saddam Hussein [did] not fully disarm, for the sake of our people and for the peace of the world, we will lead a coalition to disarm him'.[39]

The Iraqis' unenthusiastic, dilatory and limited response to UNSCR 1441 then set in train the US move to disarm them by force. If the dogs of war were champing at the bit in sections of the Bush Administration even before 1441 was passed, Iraqi obstructionism opened the gate for them inch by inch in the weeks and months that followed its passing. The Iraqis' 12,200 page dossier documenting the state and fate of the regime's banned weaponry started that process. Full of holes, replete with old material, and insistent on Iraqi innocence of the charges brought against them, the dossier was heavily criticized by the UN inspectors and fully rejected by the Bush Administration as 'anything but currently accurate, full or complete'.[40] The UN turned in consequence to its inspectors for an independent assessment of the true state of the Iraqi arsenal; and the Bush Administration moved immediately to insist that those inspectors be given access to Iraqi scientists and other witnesses outside of Iraq. Predictably, that access was not forthcoming; and for that reason among others, the first report of the renewed inspectorate, delivered to the UN on 27 January 2003, remained highly critical of levels of Iraqi cooperation and compliance. Iraq then stood condemned by the UN inspectors (and by Colin Powell) for its failure to 'come to a genuine acceptance, not even today, of the disarmament that was demanded of it';[41] and it stood condemned by other senior figures in the Bush Administration for a whole litany of sins: for the concealment and removal of weapons of mass destruction, for using its intelligence capabilities to hide its illegal arsenals, and for intimidation and coercion, obstruction and lying.[42] As the weeks passed after the vote on UNSCR 1441, Washington's patience visibly ebbed. When asked how long the UN should tolerate, and the USA would tolerate, such well-established Iraqi tactics of obfuscation and delay, Powell in December spoke only of 'a practical limit to how much longer you can just go down the road of non-cooperation'.[43] But by January even he was conceding that 'time was running out',[44] and by February President Bush was talking of the clock ticking down in 'weeks rather than months'.[45]

President Bush sent Colin Powell back to the UN on 5 February, to establish the case that Iraq was in material breach of its obligations under UNSCR 1441 and under earlier UN Security Council resolutions; and he went armed in part with supporting evidence from a UK dossier on the Iraqi regime's structures of command and deception activities issued the day before by the Blair Government in London.[46] This was effectively the multilateralists' last throw. The Iraqi regime was condemned before the UN, with a supporting panoply of photographs, documents and audio tapes, for:

- its active links to al-Qaeda through its embassy in Pakistan;
- its training of al-Qaeda members and its harbouring of a terrorist network headed by an al-Qaeda operative;
- its programme to produce ballistic missiles with a range of more than 1,200 kilometres, weapons capable of carrying chemical, biological and potentially nuclear weapons;

- its efforts to acquire key components of nuclear weapons;
- its possession of a chemical weapons facility;
- its hiding of its chemical weapons and ballistic missiles;
- its possession of mobile factories for the production of biological agents;
- its refusal to allow its scientists to speak freely to UN inspectors inside or outside Iraq;
- its systematic attempt to mislead and frustrate the returning UN inspectorate.

'Iraq has now placed itself in danger of the serious consequences called for in UNSCR 1441', Powell told the General Assembly; 'and this body places itself in danger of irrelevance if it allows Iraq to continue to defy its will without responding effectively and immediately.'[47]

It was here that the wheels began to come off the State Department's attempt to hold together its Afghanistan-style coalition in the US-orchestrated move against Iraq; and it was now that Powell began to reposition himself from dove to hawk. Major players on the UN Security Council – permanent members like Russia, China and France, and, certain of its current rotating membership, not least Germany – failed to agree with him on the immediate need to go to the military option. Instead, the inspectors asked for, and these governments supported, the granting of more time for their inspection process to work; and then, if it did not work, for the strengthening of the inspection regime by the deployment of more inspectors (and even by the deployment of supporting UN troops if necessary). Their unease at the drift of US policy, already in place prior to the passing of UNSCR 1441, was then compounded by the contents of a second and later a third report from the chief UN weapons inspector, Hans Blix, each of which reported some degree of Iraqi compliance while providing no systematic evidence of the continued existence of weapons of mass destruction. Indeed, when introducing that second report, Hans Blix actually challenged the veracity of some of Powell's evidence to the UN, calling it 'ambiguous and unconvincing'![48]

This lack of evidence only persuaded the US Administration that the inspectorate was being misled. It persuaded their critics, however, either that no such weapons existed, or that finding them required more time and resources. Inconclusive UN reports, that is, sent the USA off towards war but its critics off towards peace. It led the USA, and its UK and Spanish allies, to seek a second UN resolution, authorizing the use of force – only to have that initiative blocked by an alternative resolution, sponsored by France and Germany, one advocating a strengthened inspectorate and longer inspection period (of 120 days) instead. For a while the UK tried to play honest broker, attempting to ease French and German concerns by extending deadlines and designing new supplementary tests of Iraqi good faith. But even that could not in the end breach the deepening divide between what Secretary of Defense Rumsfeld dismissively called 'old Europe' and the 'new Europe' (Eastern European countries in the main – the so-called 'Vilnius Ten'), which was willing to back the US-led call for military intervention and regime change in Iraq. Certainly, France, Germany and Russia were not. They went public on 6 March that they would 'not let a proposed resolution pass that would authorize the use of force'. This in its turn then obliged Powell to announce publicly that such a resolution had never been necessary, and had been sought only to ease the domestic problems of some of the supporting governments, not least that of Tony Blair. Pushed on this at a press conference on 17 March, the man who only three months before had insisted that 'we will continue to work with UNMOVIC [UN Monitoring, Verification and Inspection Commission] and IAEA [International Atomic Energy Agency] and we'll consult with other members of the Council' now said:

> There can be no confusion on this point. If you remember the debate that we were having before 1441 was passed, there were some nations who insisted that a second resolution would be required. And we insisted that a second resolution would not be required. And as we negotiated our way through that, we made it absolutely clear that we did not believe that the resolution as it passed would require a second resolution. And in fact the resolution that we are not taking to a vote today is not a resolution that we believe was necessary. It was a resolution we are supporting along with the United Kingdom, who tabled it, and Spain. It was a resolution that would help some of our friends to show to their publics and the world that we had taken that one last step, we had made one last effort to see if Saddam Hussein would come into compliance.[49]

As Powell's remarks made clear, by the time the leaders of Spain, the UK and the USA gathered in the Azores in mid-March, the attempt to obtain a second UN resolution had been abandoned. Claiming now already to have all the authorization for force they required – authorization rooted in UN resolutions already passed – President Bush and Prime Ministers Blair and Aznar gave the Iraqis a last 24-hour window of opportunity, one which, when ignored, triggered first an aerial and then a ground assault on Iraq itself. It was an assault that President Bush explained to the American people in one of the fullest and clearest statements on record of why externally imposed regime change in Iraq was thought necessary. He said this.

> The Iraqi regime has used diplomacy as a ploy to gain time and advantage. It has uniformly defied Security Council resolutions demanding full disarmament. . . . Peaceful efforts to disarm the Iraqi regime have failed again and again – because we are not dealing with peaceful men. Intelligence gathered by this and other governments leaves no doubt that the Iraq regime continues to possess and conceal some of the most lethal weapons ever devised. This regime has already used weapons of mass destruction against Iraq's neighbors and against Iraq's people. The regime has a history of reckless aggression in the Middle East. It has a deep hatred of America and our friends. And it has aided, trained and harbored terrorists, including representatives of al-Qaeda.
>
> The danger is clear: using chemical, biological or, one day, nuclear weapons, obtained with the help of Iraq, the terrorists could fulfill their stated ambitions and kill thousands or hundreds of thousands of innocent people in our country, or any other. The United States and other nations did nothing to deserve or invite this threat. But we will do everything to defeat it. Instead of drifting towards tragedy, we will set a course towards safety. Before the day of horror can come, before it is too late to act, this danger will be removed.
>
> The United Stares has the sovereign authority to use force in assuring its own national security. . . . We are acting now because the risks of inaction would be far greater. In one year, or five years, the power of Iraq to inflict harm on all free nations would be multiplied many times over. With these capabilities, Saddam Hussein and his terrorist allies could choose the moment of deadly conflict when they are strongest. We choose to meet that threat now, where it arises, before it can appear suddenly in our skies and cities. . . . Terrorists and terror states do not reveal these threats with fair notice, in formal declarations – and responding to such enemies only after they have struck first is not self-defense, it is suicide. The security of the world requires disarming Saddam Hussein now.[50]

The United States went to war against Saddam Hussein, that is, on the clear understanding that the Iraqi regime was actively linked to terrorists with the global reach to attack targets in the United States. It went to war on the clear understanding that the regime possessed and was developing weapons of mass destruction; and it went to war on the clear understanding that a regime, so armed and so linked, constituted a clear and present danger to the security of the United States and to the peace of the world. 'Free nations have a duty', Bush told the American people, 'to defend our people by uniting against the violent.'[51]

Answering the Call

The manner of the UK's later involvement in the invasion of Iraq was foreshadowed – and indeed to a degree preordained – by the nature of its government's response to the events of 9/11. Like every other major government – including, it should be said, even the Iranian one – the official response from Tony Blair and his ministers to the attack on the World Trade Center and the Pentagon was one of horror, condemnation and solidarity: horror at the event, condemnation of those who perpetrated it and solidarity with the families for whom it was a personal and irreversible tragedy. But the official UK response went further than that: in five critical ways at least.

Responding to 9/11

First, and from the very beginning, the UK Government adopted this crisis as its own, and universalized its significance. Not surprisingly perhaps, in the light of the number of UK casualties, Tony Blair was quick to label the attack as 'on any basis the worse terrorist atrocity since the War perpetrated against British citizens'[1] and to link the defeat of those responsible for it directly to British national interests. 'We in Britain', he told the House of Commons in October, 'have the most direct interest in defeating such terror. It strikes at the heart of what we believe in.'[2] The Prime Minister was also quick to emphasize that the attack was not, in his view, simply an attack on the United States, or indeed on the USA and UK together, but 'an attack on civilized values everywhere'. It was, as he told the House, 'an attempt to change by terror what the terrorists knew they couldn't do by reasoned argument'.[3] The official statement from 10 Downing Street on the day of the attacks argued similarly:

> [T]his mass terrorism is the new evil in our world. The people who perpetrate it have no regard whatever for the sanctity or value of human life, and we the democracies of the world must come together to defeat it and eradicate it. This is not a battle between the United States of America and terrorism, but between the free and democratic world and terrorism. We therefore here in Britain stand shoulder to shoulder with our American friends in this hour of tragedy, and we, like them, will not rest until this evil is driven from our world.[4]

From the very beginning, that is, the UK Government treated the events of 9/11 as far more than a tragic event in a friendly state. It treated the events of 9/11 as an incident of an unprecedented and epochal kind that was of direct interest to the UK itself, and it signed up to a global campaign to prevent its repetition. This was not, Tony Blair told Larry King in November 2001, 'a fight that Britain could stay out of, even if we wanted to', since 'it involves all of us and all people who believe in the same values of freedom and tolerance and respect for other people and the peaceful way of life'.[5]

Second, and linked to that, the UK Government moved immediately to position itself alongside the US Administration – 'shoulder to shoulder' in Tony Blair's words – as an architect and leading player in the design and implementation of the global anti-terrorism campaign. In this regard, it was significant (and was immediately understood to be significant) that Tony Blair was the only major world leader present in the audience when President Bush spoke to the American people and the world from Capitol Hill on 20 September. For the Prime Minister was clear from the outset that the UK would stand full-square with the USA both in its grief and in its response to the attacks. He was also clear from the outset that – without denying that this would inevitably and properly be a US-led campaign – the UK intended to play far more than a supporting role in the emerging alliance against al-Qaeda: that his government was willing actively to engage in the design and implementation of a joint US/UK response to the events of 9/11. It was for this reason that the UK mobilized militarily alongside the USA as the Bush Administration prepared to take on the Taliban, with the RAF playing a major supporting role in the air campaign and UK ground troops providing the first core of the coalition forces that policed post-Taliban Kabul. At the press conference that preceded his trip to New York late in September 2001, Tony Blair was pressed on the degree of this renewed US/UK closeness. This was his response:

I think that the best way of answering that is to say that from the very outset there has been very, very close cooperation between ourselves and the US in every aspect of this, whether it is military, diplomatic or political, so we have been working very carefully together.[6]

Moreover, in this process of sustaining what Tony Blair would later describe as a 'remarkable ... degree of accord and agreement between us and the Americans',[7] the UK Government entirely absorbed from the outset what came to be the central defining features of the US response. It came to accept that what was happening here was a war, and a war against an enemy defined only through the blanket label of 'terrorist'. It also came to accept that, since what was going on here was a war, the correct response to the attacks on 9/11 would be military and punitive, and would be directed not simply at the terrorists but at their supporters. It came to accept too that being now at war, the response to the events of 9/11 was likely to be a long one – an affair of stages, with developing and changing targets throughout – and one that would be finally finished only with the full destruction of the terrorist networks whose attacks had triggered it. Only days after President Bush labelled the post-9/11 world as one that was at war, Tony Blair also settled into that language. He told CNN that 'yes, whatever the technical or legal issues about the declaration of war, the fact is that we are at war with terrorism'. He reassured his predominantly American audience both that there had 'to be a response to bring those terrorists who committed the attack to account; and that we [the British] will play our full part in that'.[8] 'We are completely committed to seeing this thing through.'[9] He also told the House of Commons that 'even when al-Qaeda is dealt with, the job is not over. The network of terrorism is not confined to it';[10] and he told Larry King that al-Qaeda was something that 'you defeat ... you can't negotiate with them ... you just defeat them. You just eradicate the whole network'.[11]

Fourth, from the very outset, New Labour gave to this first phase of military action after 9/11 a high moral purpose. Tony Blair presented the preparations for a military response to the events of 9/11 as the preparations for a *just* war: a war whose underlying morality had multiple sources. The war was just because the enemy was an organization of fanatics. 'This is a war ... between the civilized world and fanaticism', he said.[12] It was not, he insisted, a war between 'the West and the Arab world, or the West and Islam'.[13] On the contrary, as he told the Arab journalists when questioned on this very point in October 2001:

The last time I was engaged in military action of this nature was in Kosovo, protecting hundreds of thousands of innocent refugees that were in fact Muslims against ethnic cleansing that was being undertaken by a dictatorial regime in a country that was in fact . . . Christian. . . . For us, this is a matter of justice.[14]

The war was also just, in Blair's view, because the attack had been unprovoked, and had involved the slaughter of the innocent. It was a morally justified war because its adversaries were themselves devoid of morality. 'These people', he told CNN, 'if they could do worse, would do worse; the number of people they kill is not limited by anything other than pure technical capacity.'[15] Indeed, the protection of the innocent from slaughter of this kind rapidly became a key theme in the UK Government's description of its preparation for the military overthrow of the Taliban. 'We are also working as hard as we can', Tony Blair told Arab journalists in October 2001, 'on the humanitarian side of this', and not just on the military one.[16] The war was just, so the argument ran, because it would be accompanied by a serious effort at humanitarian aid; and it was just because it would be followed by a sustained effort to create a stable and democratic Afghanistan. 'This time we will not walk away from you', the Prime Minister told the Afghan people; 'we have given commitments. We will honour those commitments, both on the humanitarian side and in terms of rebuilding Afghanistan.'[17]

Finally, the military action that overthrew the Taliban was justified by UK ministers, both when it was designed and when it was implemented, in the language of coalition. From the very beginning, Tony Blair emphasized the width (and the importance of the width) of the group of countries that were actively supporting US and UK military action in Afghanistan. He also stressed the importance of a major UN presence in the rebuilding process. 'The whole of Europe will stand with America on this', he told Larry King; 'the whole of the civilized world will stand together.' And it was only right and proper that they would do so because:

we must put together a broad-based coalition to hound these people down and bring them to account, and do it . . . for reasons of justice. We owe it to those people that lost their lives, to their families who are grieving, and to our own defence of democracy and liberty and freedom.[18]

Accordingly, the UK Government set great store by the fact that, 'in addition to Britain, France, Germany, Australia and Canada . . . had all pledged military support . . . the EU is fully supportive' and that in 'Russia ... China ... Japan ... Pakistan ... India ... [and] the Arab world there has been widespread condemnation of the 11 September atrocities and acceptance of the need to take action against the al-Qaeda network'.[19] What by contrast the UK Government did not accept was any accusation that it was exercising a double standard here: being tough on an anti-terror campaign in Afghanistan but soft on efforts to put an end to attacks on Israel and incursions into Palestinian territories. In October 2001, Arab journalists pressed Tony Blair on what was then a widely held view in the Middle East and beyond, but he would have none of it. 'Nothing', he told them, 'could ever possibly justify the 11 September attacks'; and as to the peace process in the Middle East, 'we work on this constantly'.[20]

   Significantly however, in the light of what was to follow, the UK Government's response to equally probing and regular questions about a second stage of this campaign, and a second country (namely Iraq), was opaque from the start. With the exception of an initial Foreign Office denial of any Iraqi involvement in the events of 9/11, UK Government statements on the future fate of Iraq were – throughout the Afghan phase of this story – remarkable for their impenetrability. Post-9/11, UK leaders did not deny that the campaign would have a second stage; but during the Afghan stage of the campaign they would not be drawn on the specifics of its focus and character. When asked specifically by journalists in New York in September 2001, 'Where do you see Iraq in all this? Are they in or are they out?' all that Tony Blair would say was that 'we have made it clear all the way through-out that we proceed on the basis of evidence'.[21] When asked in October if he was 'considering a new way of dealing with Iraq', he chose to restrict his answer to a discussion of 'a new regime for sanctions';[22] and when pushed in December 2001 on whether 'Britain would see itself playing a role against al-Qaeda cells in places such as Somalia, or Sudan or possibly against Iraq', the Prime Minister (with Colin Powell standing alongside him) talked only in general and procedural terms, saying that:

> in respect of Phase 2 I have really got nothing to add to what I have said throughout. We have concentrated on achieving our objectives in Afghanistan. Of course, the battle against international terrorism does not end there, but we will proceed by way of deliberation and con-sideration with key strategic partners and allies; and of course Britain stands willing to play its part in that.[23]

There are pages and pages of Blair's speeches on Afghanistan between September and December 2001: but on Iraq in that period there are hardly any public statements at all.

Standing 'Shoulder to Shoulder'

This changed (because it had to change) after George W. Bush's State of the Union address to Congress in January 2002. That address put Iraq fully in the spotlight of the 'war against terrorism', and rapidly obliged the UK Government, as the US's closest and most active ally in the war against the Taliban, to take a public position on Iraq as well.

The first formulations of the public position came from the Foreign Secretary. In a series of speeches that began in February, Jack Straw advocated what he termed 'a diplomacy of foresight'. Reflecting on the lessons of 11 September, and paying specific attention to the abuses of human rights in Iraq, he argued strongly that 'UK best interests are best served by an active and engaged global foreign policy, working with our allies to push back' what he called 'the boundaries of chaos'. It was not, he argued, that the UK was any more a superpower. It was rather that it still had 'a pivotal role' to play in global policy-making: not least by finding ways in which the international community could 'stand up to bullies like Saddam, and not leave these problems to the next generation to sort out'.[24] Indeed, by April the UK Foreign Secretary was insisting that 'blatant contempt for international law [could] never be regarded [purely] as an internal matter', and that 'nowhere [was] this more pertinent than Iraq'; and by April too, Jack Straw was laying down general principles to guide policy for peace and prosperity in the modern global community: four principles in fact, the last of which embodied this new and pre-emptive diplomacy of foresight:

> First, that international relations must be founded on the idea that every nation has an obligation properly to meet its global responsibilities.
>
> Second, that the global community has the right to make judgments about countries' internal affairs, where they flout or fail to abide by these global values.
>
> Third, because our interests as nation states are now more entwined than ever, the global community must make renewed efforts to resolve those persistent conflicts which threaten the security of us all.
>
> And fourth, that the global community must play a more active role in dealing with conflicts within states, which in the past have been overlooked until too late.[25]

By then, his Prime Minister was in Texas, meeting the world's press in the company of the younger President Bush, and speaking in the Presidential Library named for the senior one. In both the press conference and the speech, the main lines of the UK's emerging policy on Iraq became clearer still, as Blair identified himself closely with the view that Iraq *was* indeed the next problem in the war on terrorism, and emphasized his Government's preference for a UN-focused and diplomatic resolution to the threat that Iraq was now said to pose. Both the manner of Blair's specification of the Iraqi threat and its resolution are worth considering in detail; for in April those specifications, though broadly in line with those of the American administration, were not entirely congruent with them.

When asked directly in the press conference whether the UK was with the USA in 'targeting' Saddam Hussein, the Blair response was cautious indeed – so cautious in fact that it drew an unscripted response from George Bush himself. The exchange went as follows.

QUESTION Prime Minister, we have heard the President say what his policy is directly about Saddam Hussein: which is to remove him. . . . Could I ask you whether that is now the policy of the British Government?

BLAIR You know that it has always been our policy that Iraq would be a better place without Saddam Hussein. I don't think anyone should be in any doubt about that for all the reasons I gave earlier . . . reasons to do with weapons of mass destruction, also to do with the appalling brutality and repression of his own people. But how we now proceed in this situation, how we make sure that this threat that is posed by weapons of mass destruction is dealt with, that is open. And when the time comes for taking those decisions, we will tell people about those decisions. But you cannot have a situation in which he carries on being in breach of UN resolutions and refusing to allow us the capability of assessing how that weapons of mass destruction capability is being advanced, even though the international community has made it clear that he should do so. Now, as I say, how we then proceed from there, that is a matter that is open to us.

BUSH Maybe I should be a little less direct and be a little more nuanced, and say we support regime change.[26]

If there was a 'Blair doctrine/position' at this point in the developing story, it was one laid out in more systematic form in the speech that followed two days later. It was a position combining the advocacy of an active and interventionist foreign policy with a clear preference for a resolution of the Iraqi issue by multilaterally-based diplomacy, as part of a wider Middle East settlement. It was also a position that left the UK open to the case that Iraq was a legitimate target for active interventionism; and one that for the moment ducked the issue of whether such activism should and could be pursued if multilateral diplomacy either failed or could not be mobilized. As Blair presented it in Texas, active interventionism by countries like the USA and the UK was contingent on the existence of a genuine threat, so the logic of the argument that took him into unilateral alliance with the USA later was already there: buried, not faced as yet, but already present in the way the argument was put. If the threat was big enough, and the international community could not be mobilized against it, then active interventionism would have to be done unilaterally.

But that would become clear only much later. For the moment, and in a speech in which Tony Blair also called for renewed efforts to broker a broader Middle East settlement and welcomed the Bush Administration's belated public commitment to a two-state solution to the Israeli-Palestinian conflict, the UK Prime Minister had this to say about the need for an active foreign policy of the kind pursued in Kosovo:

> I advocate an enlightened self-interest that puts fighting for our values at the heart of the policies necessary to protect our nations. Engage-ment in the world on the basis of these values, not isolationism from it, is the hard-headed pragmatism for the 21st century. Why? In part . . . because the countries and people of the world today are more interdependent than ever . . . and of course the surest way to stability is through the very values of freedom, democracy and justice. Where these are strong, the people push for moderation and order. Where they are absent, regimes act unchecked by popular accountability and pose a threat: and the threat spreads. So the promotion of these values becomes not just right in itself but part of our long-term security and prosperity. Not all the wrongs of the world can be put right, but where disorder threatens us all, we should act. . . . We cannot, of course, intervene in all cases, but where countries are engaged in the terror or weapons of mass destruction business, we should not shrink from confronting them.

On Iraq and the 'axis of evil', he said this:

> I hope in time that Syria, Iran and even North Korea can accept the need to change their relations dramatically with the outside world. A new relationship is on offer. But they must know that sponsoring terrorism or weapons of mass destruction is not acceptable. As for Iraq, I know some fear precipitate action. They needn't. We will pro-ceed, as we did after September 11, in a calm, measured, sensible but firm way. But leaving Iraq to develop weapons of mass destruction,

in flagrant breach of no less than nine separate UN Security Council resolutions, refusing still to allow weapons inspectors back to do their work properly, is not an option. . . . As I say, the moment for decision on how to act is not yet with us. But to allow weapons of mass destruction to be developed by a state like Iraq without let or hindrance would be grossly to ignore the lessons of September 11 and we will not do it. The message to Saddam is clear: he has to let the inspectors back in – anyone, any time, any place that the international community demands.[27]

The other element in the UK's emerging response to the US linking of Iraq to terrorism was a powerful insistence by London on the making by the Bush Administration of a second linkage too: that between policy on Iraq and policy on Palestine. This was very much the stuff of Tony Blair's conversation with George Bush in Texas in April – when the US President had briefly publicly criticized the Israeli Government for its military incursions into Palestinian-controlled parts of the West Bank – and it was a theme in every major foreign policy speech made by Jack Straw throughout 2002. The *Guardian* later gave this description of the importance of this issue at the very highest levels of UK Government in the build-up to the military action against Iraq:

Cabinet debate was reborn in September . . . meetings up to that date tended to be tame affairs. That changed when Mr Blair spoke to cabinet colleagues on Iraq, the day he was due to address MPs recalled from their summer break to discuss the issue. As the discussion went round the table, it was Palestine, Palestine, Palestine. There was a consensus that the Israeli-Palestinian issue had to be dealt with in tandem with Iraq, or preferably before. . . . Mr Blair told colleagues that the potential Achilles Heel of his Iraq strategy was the Palestinian-Israeli issue. He said that he was clear that movement in the peace process had to be made in parallel with Iraq, otherwise resentment in the Arab world against the West would fester.[28]

So from as early as April 2002 the UK Government pressed the US Administration both to take the UN route to the containment of the Iraqi 'threat', and to twin-track its pressure on Iraq with pressure on Israel to negotiate a viable peace settlement with the Palestinians. But as the months passed, US willingness to do the latter visibly diminished, in the face of the continuing Intifada and the intransigence of the Sharon Government. The battle within the US Administration, as we have seen, was less over Israel than over whether the UN route was one worth taking in relation to Iraq; and on this at least, the UK was initially more successful as a lobbyist and an ally. British pressure played a key role in reinforcing the views of the 'doves' within the Administration – views that held sway throughout 2002 and eventually triggered the passing of UNSCR 1441.[29] UK ministers were rarely explicit on this as their purpose; but very occasionally the truth and importance of this role came out. 'If Tony had gone off and done a Schroeder,' as one of his colleagues put it, 'we would have had no influence.'[30] So Tony Blair had this to say to a gathering of British ambassadors in London in January 2003:

> First, we should remain the closest ally of the US, and as allies influence them to continue broadening their agenda. . . . We share their values and . . . it is massively in our self-interest to remain close allies . . . but we should use this alliance to good effect. The problem people have with the US . . . is that . . . they want the US to listen back. So for the international community . . . global poverty is important, global warming is important, the UN is important. The US choice to go through the UN over Iraq was a vital step in itself and a symbol of the desire to work with others. A broader agenda is not inimical to the US. . . . The price of British influence is not, as some would have it, that we have obediently to do what the US asks. . . . The price of influence is that we do not leave the US to face the tricky issues alone. . . . International terrorism is one such issue. Weapons of Mass Destruction are another.[31]

Building a Multilateral Alliance

A further price of that influence was that the UK Government needed to be as active in pursuing a new UN resolution as it wanted the US Administration to be; and it certainly was. For the rest of 2002, the UK Government left no stone unturned in its public campaign to build support – both domestically and globally – for a new UN resolution demanding the immediate and untrammelled return of a strengthened weapons inspectorate to Iraq. When Tony Blair joined George Bush at Camp David in September – the meeting later singled out by his critics as the one at which he accepted the case for military intervention – he took the opportunity to brief the attending press corps on the dangers presented by Saddam Hussein and on the need for real and decisive action by the UN. In relation to Iraq, he said:

> What we know from what has been going on there for a long period of time is not just the chemical, biological weapons capability, but we know that they were trying to develop nuclear weapons capability. . . .

there is a real issue that has to be tackled here. . . . I was just reading coming over here the catalogue of attempts by Iraq to conceal its weapons of mass destruction, not to tell the truth about it over – not just over a period of months, but over a period of years. Now that's why the issue is important. And of course it's an issue not just for America, not just for Britain, it's an issue for the whole of the international community. But it is an issue we have to deal with. And that's why I say to you that the policy of inaction, doing nothing about it, is not something we can responsibly adhere to.[32]

Jack Straw laid out the UK case against Saddam Hussein's Iraq in speeches in the UK and before the UN in September 2002. It was a case built, as Tony Blair's had been at Camp David, around the special evils and dangers of the regime itself, and around the threat that its continuation posed to the credibility of the UN as an institution. This was Straw speaking in Birmingham:

No other country but Iraq has so persistently undermined the UN charter and the authority of the Security Council. No other country but Iraq has annexed a fellow UN member state. No other country but Iraq poses the same unique threat to the integrity of international law. No other country but Iraq has the same appetite for developing and for using weapons of mass destruction. Until Iraq meets its UN obligations to the full, there can be no guarantee that it will not use chemical, biological or even nuclear weapons. The burden of proof is on Saddam. It would be wildly irresponsible to argue that patience with Iraq should be unlimited, or that military action should not be an option. Until the international community faces up to the threat represented by Iraq's weapons of mass destruction, we place at risk the lives of civilians in the region and beyond.[33]

The UK accordingly sought a renewed UN mandate for international inspection of the Iraqi military arsenal, and advocated a combination of multilateralism and the threat of force. As Jack Straw put it: 'if any new resolution is to have real effect, it must be backed with the credible threat of force. The Iraqi regime should be left under no illusion of the consequences of non-compliance or the depth of our resolve.'[34] To that end, the UK Government drew up its own dossier on the threat supposedly posed to western security by the Iraqi regime's development of weapons of mass destruction, and then used every public opportunity it could to keep awareness of that threat before the British public. By the time the dossier *Iraq's Weapons of Mass Destruction: The Assessment of the British Government* was published on 24 September, the UK case against Iraq had crystallized into the following set of propositions – none of which, as it happened, had much to say about the link to al-Qaeda that was supposed to have triggered the original shift of emphasis in the war on terrorism from Afghanistan to Iraq. By September 2002, the UK case against the Iraqi regime was primarily a human rights and weapons of mass destruction one, as follows:

- With the Taliban gone, the Iraqi regime was 'revealed as the world's worst regime: brutal, dictatorial, with a wretched human rights record',[35] that included systematic rape and torture, barbaric punishments and summary executions, and a willingness to use chemical weapons on its own people.
- As recently as 1998, when the UN inspectorate withdrew, the Iraqi regime remained in possession of 'enough chemical and biological weapons . . . to devastate the entire Gulf region'.[36] Some of these weapons, according to the dossier, were capable of deployment within 45 minutes of an order to use them.[37] The dossier also pointed to the post-1991 rebuilding of old factories and building of new facilities that were capable of being used to produce such weapons.
- The Iraqi regime was secretly developing a nuclear weapons programme that, if successful in its pursuit of materials, could produce weapons within one to two years. There was evidence – from intelligence sources – that the regime was intensifying its efforts to acquire the materials necessary for the production of nuclear weapons; and that, in particular, 'Iraq has sought significant quantities of uranium from Africa, despite having no active civil nuclear power programme that could require it'.[38]
- The regime, according to the dossier, was also currently hiding up to twenty Scud missiles with a range of 650 kilometres, and was possibly working on a rocket capable of flying over 1,000 kilometres (and as such, into south-eastern Europe itself). The dossier suggested the possibility of the use of such rockets to deliver chemical and biological warheads (though it could produce no evidence that such warheads had yet been made).
- Possession of these weapons, the development of these programmes, and the ejection of the UN inspectorate in 1998 put the regime in defiance of binding UN resolutions. Tony Blair mentioned '23 such obligations' in his address to the TUC (Trades Union Congress) in 2002.
- The policy of containment, represented by the no-fly zones and the embargo on oil sales, was not now fully effective and in any case could not go on indefinitely.

From this case, the UK Government in the autumn of 2002 drew two major conclusions. The first was that time and evidence were no longer on the side of those arguing for a continuation of the existing policy of containment: the need now was for the full disarmament of the Iraqi regime, not its containment. The second was that the appropriate body to oversee that disarmament was the UN: a UN equipped with a renewed mandate and one backed by the credible threat of military action if required.

Again, the words are important. Tony Blair wrote this about the new intelligence information of which he was now in regular receipt, and which clearly figured centrally in his own calculations on appropriate courses of action:

> In recent months I have been increasingly alarmed by the evidence from inside Iraq that despite sanctions, despite the damage done to his capability in the past, despite the UN Security Council Resolutions expressly outlawing it, and despite his denials, Saddam Hussein is continuing to develop weapons of mass destruction, and with them the ability to inflict real damage upon the region and the stability of the world. . . . What I believe the assessed intelligence has established beyond doubt is that Saddam has continued to produce chemical and biological weapons, that he continues in his efforts to develop nuclear weapons, and that he has been able to extend the range of his ballistic missile programme. I also believe that . . . Saddam will now do his utmost to try to conceal his weapons from UN inspectors. . . . I am in no doubt that the threat is serious and current, that he has made progress on weapons of mass destruction, and that he has to be stopped. . . . We must ensure that he does not get to use the weapons he has, or get hold of the weapons he wants.[39]

In presenting the dossier to the House of Commons on 24 September, Tony Blair also addressed directly those who asked 'but why Saddam?', 'why now?' and 'why should Britain care?':

> [W]hy Saddam? I don't in the least dispute there are other causes of concern on weapons of mass destruction . . . but two things about Saddam stand out. He has used these weapons . . . and his is a regime with no moderate elements to appeal to. Read the chapter on Saddam and human rights. . . . Read it all and again I defy anyone to say that this cruel and sadistic dictator should be allowed any possibility of getting his hands on more chemical, biological or even nuclear weapons.
>
> Why now? People ask. I agree I cannot say that this month or next, this year or next, that he will use his weapons. But I can say that if the international community, having made the call for his disarmament, now . . . shrugs its shoulders and walks away, he will draw the conclusion

dictators faced with a weakening will, always draw. . . . He will carry on, his efforts will intensify, his confidence will grow and at some point, in a future not too distant, the threat will turn into reality . . .

And if people say, why should Britain care? I answer: because there is no way that this man, in this region above all regions, could begin a conflict using such weapons and the conflict not engulf the whole world.[40]

Going Alone

With the passing of UNSCR 1441 the twin lines of UK policy in Iraq had their moment of greatest success: Iraq was recognized as a rogue state in need of externally imposed disarmament, and the international community was, for the moment at least, formally united in its determination to see that disarmament achieved. But by the same token UNSCR 1441 put the ball firmly in the Iraqi court. As Tony Blair told the guests at the Lord Mayor's Banquet in November 2002, 'the dispute is with Saddam. It is now up to him how it is resolved: by peace or by conflict'.[41]

As we saw in the previous chapter, the parameters set around Saddam Hussein's regime by the resolution, and by the interpretation of its terms insisted upon both in London and in Washington, were very tight. Tony Blair spelt them out in the House of Commons in November:

> This resolution sets up a tough new inspection regime. . . . The duty of Saddam Hussein is to cooperate fully and totally. This means giving access to all the sites and palaces. It means allowing key witnesses to be interviewed free from fear. It means a full declaration of the weapons that exist and their whereabouts. The obligation is to cooperate. It is not a game of hide and seek. . . . The duty of cooperation means not just access but information. Failure to be open and honest in helping the inspectors do their work is every much a breach as failure to allow access to sites. If Saddam complies, that is the UN mandate fulfilled.[42]

But Blair also assured the House that day that non-compliance would not automatically trigger military action. What it would trigger would be a second resolution. The threat of force was there, but so too was the insistence that regime change would not be imposed if cooperation was forthcoming. Again, the words are important, because their inflection is so different from those of Rumsfeld and Wolfowitz:

To those who fear this resolution is just an automatic trigger point, without any further discussion point, paragraph 12 of the resolution makes it clear that it is not. But everyone now accepts that if there is a default by Saddam, the international community must act to enforce its will. Saddam must now make his choice. My message to him is this: disarm or you face force. There must be no more games, no more deceit, no more prevarication, obstruction or defiance. Cooperate fully and, despite the terrible injustice you have often inflicted on others, we will be just with you. But defy the UN's will and we will disarm you by force. Be under no doubt whatever of that.[43]

As the weeks passed, however, and that cooperation was not forthcoming – certainly not forthcoming in anything like the quantity and speed that both London and Washington required – the wheels began to come off the UK strategy of disarming Iraq through multi-lateral international action. By January 2003, the Bush Administration was already running out of patience – the President actually made his 'weeks, not months' remark when standing next to Tony Blair in London – and the British were soon scrambling for a second UN resolution to legitimate the use of force.[44] Labour ministers were also by then having to scramble at home, to persuade an increasingly sceptical electorate about the wisdom of any rush to war, UN-legiti-mated or not. In that scramble, ministers began heavily to deploy three arguments in defence of military action against Iraq that had hitherto played a less central role in the public debate: an argument about the nature of the links between the Iraqi regime and terrorism; an argument about the dangers of appeasement; and an argument about the moral case for regime change. If we are to understand why and how the UK Government eventually went to war alongside the USA – and did not stand shoulder to shoulder with its main European allies – we need to recognize the substance and importance of all three of these newly important justificatory claims.

On the *linkage* side of the case, Labour ministers in the first months of 2003 found themselves pressed repeatedly about whether any such links existed at all. The credibility of their second dossier on Iraq, issued in February, was heavily compromised by the discovery that some of its content had been plagiarized from an academic article published in the *Middle East Review of International Affairs* (initial press reports had made things worse by giving the source as a doc-toral thesis written 12 years earlier). Robin Cook later characterized the issuing of that dossier by the Government as an enormously dam-aging self-inflicted wound, calling it 'a glorious, spectacular own goal'.[45] The Government's general claims about the direct linkage between Iraq and terrorism were then weakened still further by Tony

Blair's admission in the House that although there were 'unquestion-ably' links between al-Qaeda and Iraq, 'how far the links go is a matter of speculation'.[46] And since it was, ministers were increasingly obliged to fall back onto the argument of an *indirect* linkage between Saddam Hussein and al-Qaeda: onto an argument about the dangers of 'international terrorism and weapons of mass destruction' coming 'together because they threaten the peace and order and stability of the world'. 'We should realize', Blair said in January 2003, with George Bush by his side, 'those two threats – terrorism, weapons of mass destruction – are not different. They are linked, and dealing with them both is essential for the future peace and security and prosperity of the world.'[47] Why? Because:

> I have got absolutely no doubt at all that unless we deal with both of these threats, they will come together in a deadly form . . . terrorism and weapons of mass destruction are linked dangers. States which are failed, which repress their people brutally, in which notions of demo-cracy and the rule of law are alien, *share the same absence of rational boundaries to their actions* as the terrorist. Iraq has used weapons of mass destruction. . . . Just reflect on it and the danger is clear.[48]

On the timing issue, in the early months of 2003, as opposition to their policy intensified at home, Labour ministers were increasingly obliged in addition to play the *appeasement* card. They began to stress repeatedly the 'twelve years of procrastination and deception' argument to show why the UN inspectorate strategy for which they had pressed so hard in November was not likely to succeed. They began to talk of inspections only working because of the deployment of troops offshore; and they began to argue – as the Security Council deadlocked and the chances of a second resolution slipped away – of the dangers of sending Saddam Hussein a message of weakness. As Jack Straw put it:

> If we fail to back our words with deeds, we follow one of the most catastrophic precedents in history. The descent into war in the 1930s is a searing reminder of the dangers of turning a blind eye while inter-national law is subverted by the law of the jungle. . . . If the Security Council were to demonstrate that it was incapable of tackling the new threats of weapons of mass destruction and terrorism, it would risk doing as much damage to the UN as that suffered by the League of Nations when it failed to face up to the challenges of the 1930s. In failing to hold Saddam to account, other would-be proliferators would rightly draw the conclusion that our commitment to prevent the spread of the world's deadliest weapons amounted to empty rhetoric.[49]

In fact, by February 2003 so strong was the opposition to the UK's slippage into unilateral military action with the United States that Tony Blair began increasingly to turn to a third, and *moral*, argument for military intervention. Against the background of growing demands within the Security Council for the inspectors to be given more time and more resources, and on the day on which a million protesters filled the streets of London,[50] the Prime Minister wrote this in the columns of the Sunday paper that many of them were likely to read that weekend:

> I continue to want to solve the issue of Iraq and weapons of mass destruction through the UN. . . . But . . . no one seriously believes that Saddam is yet cooperating fully. In all honesty, most people don't really believe he ever will. So what holds people back? What brings thousands of people out in protests around the world? And let's not pretend that in March or April or May or June people will feel different. It is not really an issue of timing or 200 inspectors versus 100. It is a right and entirely understandable hatred of war. It is moral purpose, and I respect that.
>
> But the moral case against war has a moral answer: it is the moral case for removing Saddam. *It is not the reason we act. That must be according to the UN mandate on weapons of mass destruction.* But it is the reason, frankly, why if we do have to act, we should do so with a clear conscience.
>
> Yes there are consequences of war . . . but there are also consequences of 'stop the war'. There will be no march for the victims of Saddam, no protests about the thousands of children who die needlessly each year under his rule, no righteous anger over the torture chambers which, if he is left in power, will remain in being. . . . If there are 500,000 on the [Stop the War] march, that is less than the number of people whose deaths Saddam has been responsible for. If there are one million, that is still less than the number of people who died in the wars he started. So if the result of peace is Saddam staying in power, not disarmed, then I tell you there are consequences paid in blood for that decision too. But these victims will never be seen, never feature on our TV screens or inspire millions to take to the streets. But they will exist nonetheless.[51]

Alone at Home

But even arguments of that force did little to stem the tide of opposition that built up within the ranks of the Labour Party over the winter of 2002–3, or to reverse the drift of public opinion away from support for military action and for Tony Blair. Popular and political support for action under UN mandate remained; but opposition grew to any move towards unilateral action based on arguments about terrorism, weapons of mass destruction and the threat to UK security supposedly posed by the Iraqi regime.[52] There had always been a residue of opposition. In September 2001, 53 Labour MPs had voted against the Government's policy on Iraq. In November 2002, the rebels had numbered 32. And there were regular reports throughout the winter of unease in particular Government departments – particularly the Foreign Office – and among unnamed cabinet ministers. But by February 2003 the scale of opposition had grown far higher. It had grown publicly far higher, in that demonstrations against the war now recruited in their tens and hundreds of thousands; and it had grown politically far higher (within the ranks of the parliamentary Labour Party itself). When MPs were twice called upon to vote in support of Government policy in the run up to the invasion, the number of dissenters within Labour backbench ranks grew on each occasion: in February to 121 and in March to 139. In March, some 20 Labour MPs also abstained. By March 2003 Government policy had also triggered ministerial resignations: first, five parliamentary private secretaries and three junior ministers, and then the architect of the Kosovo campaign himself, the former Foreign Secretary, Robin Cook. Clare Short followed Cook out of the cabinet in May.

Robin Cook announced his resignation on 17 March 2003, the eve of the vote in the House of Commons on the use of military action, explaining: 'I cannot support a war without international agreement or domestic support.' While he applauded the 'heroic efforts' that Tony Blair had made in pursuing a second resolution, he argued that Britain 'is being asked to embark on a war without agreement in any of the international bodies of which we are a leading partner'. Referring to the aftermath of 9/11, he said:

> Only a year ago, we and the United States were part of a coalition against terrorism that was wider and more diverse than I would ever have imagined possible. History will be astonished at the diplomatic miscalculations that led so quickly to the disintegration of that powerful coalition. The US can afford to go it alone, but Britain is not a superpower. Our interests are best protected not by unilateral action but by multilateral agreement and a world order governed by rules.

He also pointed out the paradox at the heart of the argument of the security threat posed by Saddam Hussein: 'Ironically, it is only because Iraq's military forces are so weak that we can even contemplate its invasion', and 'we cannot base our military strategy on the assumption that Saddam is weak and at the same time justify pre-emptive action on the claim that he is a threat'.[53]

But by then reasoned opposition of this kind was to no avail. Faced with the patent incapacity of either the USA or the UK to win a second UN resolution authorizing the use of force against Iraq, and with 45,000 UK ground troops already mobilized for that attack, Tony Blair's cabinet colleagues crossed their own particular Rubicon in the wake of the Azores meeting of 17 March. They switched tack – Jack Straw apparently only just[54] – abandoned their attempt to win a second resolution, belatedly discovered to their own satisfaction (if not necessarily to everyone else's) that UNSCR 1441 was sufficient to make their action internationally legal, and threw in their lot with the Bush Administration. Tony Blair let it be known that 'he would resign rather than countenance a refusal by the Commons to send British troops into action to disarm Saddam Hussein without UN consent';[55] and then lobbied hard to survive the largest backbench rebellion of his premiership thus far. On his orders, UK planes, which had long flown with American fighters over Iraq's no-fly zones, now joined the all-out air campaign against Iraq proper, and on 21 March UK troops crossed the Iraqi border in a military campaign that took them into, and eventually gave them control of, Iraq's second city, Basra. They went with this Churchillian statement from their Prime Minister circulating to the nation:

Tonight, British servicemen and women are engaged from air, land and sea. Their mission: to remove Saddam Hussein from power, and disarm Iraq of its weapons of mass destruction. . . . Should terrorists obtain these weapons being manufactured and traded around the world, the carnage they could inflict to our economies, our security, to world peace, would be beyond our most vivid imagination. My judgement, as Prime Minister, is that this threat is real, growing, and of an entirely different nature to any conventional threat to our security that Britain has faced before. For twelve years the world tried to disarm Saddam; after his wars in which hundreds of thousands died, UN weapons inspectors say vast amounts of chemical and biological poisons . . . remain unaccounted for in Iraq. So our choice is clear: back down and leave Saddam hugely strengthened; or proceed to disarm him by force. Retreat might give us a moment of respite, but years of repentance at our weakness would, I believe, follow. It is true Saddam is not the only threat. But it is true also – as we British know – that the best way to deal with future threats peacefully is to deal with present threats with resolve. . . . Dictators like Saddam, terrorist groups like al-Qaeda, threaten the very existence of a world [of stability and order that is vital to the resolution of the other] challenges that confront us – peace in the Middle East . . . poverty, the environment, the ravages of disease. . . . That is why I have asked our troops to go into action tonight. As so often before, on the courage and determination of British men and women, serving our country, the fate of many nations rests.[56]

PART II

WHY THE WAR HAPPENED

The Justifications for War

As we have now seen at every stage in the unfolding drama of New Labour and Iraq, an operation of this enormity and significance clearly required extensive justification. After all, it was no minor thing to mobilize a huge army in a democratic society, and then to deploy it in a unilateral invasion of another state's territory. It was also no minor thing to set about 'regime change' there in the face of sustained opposition from the vast majority of other major governments, and at the cost of dividing the invading powers from the support of the bulk of those countries which normally stand in ideological and military alliance with them. For as we have seen, unlike the first Gulf War in 1991, this second military move against Saddam Hussein's Iraq went ahead without explicit UN approval. Unlike the war of 1991, it split NATO, divided the European Union, alienated the bulk of the Arab world and – in an ironic commentary on these post-Cold War days – actually left the two leading NATO powers at the head of a 'coalition of the willing' that contained more former Warsaw Pact members than it did NATO ones.[1] So the invasion of Iraq clearly needed considerable justification from those triggering it; and of course, as we have now seen in detail and at length, it received that justification on a daily basis and in considerable volume.

For our purposes here, two features of the justificatory structure that preceded and then accompanied the invasion are particularly worthy of note. The first is that the justifications that were addressed directly to the issue of Iraq varied in content, and shifted in priority over time, and did so as the relative viability of individual justificatory arguments rose and fell in the face of available evidence and shifting public concerns. The second feature of the justificatory arguments worthy of note here is that the theses addressed directly to Iraq gathered their force, for those who made them, in part at least because of their relationship to a wider and more indirect set of arguments (and justifications for military action) that were neither Iraqi-triggered nor necessarily Iraqi-specific. In this 'indirect' sense, Iraq was legitimated as a target because the USA had been attacked by a group of Islamic terrorists who had emerged from a world that was no longer organized along, and controlled by, Cold War tensions. Iraq was legitimated as a target because that Cold War division of the world had been replaced by a new division between western values and fundamentalist Islam, a division on whose fault line Iraq itself had the misfortune to stand. It was this need to police the fault line that actually made Iraq so central to the thinking of at least certain sections of the Bush Administration; and it was in the gap between their realpolitik and New Labour's naivety that much of the dynamic of this story was ultimately rooted.

In the wake of the war, the justificatory structure deployed to initiate and sustain it was increasingly subject to attack. Charge and countercharge flowed back and forth between the war's advocates and their critics, in exchanges that generated elements of light over time, but also immense quantities of heat. Because of the exchanges, we do already know more than we did at the time about the thinking that led to the invasion. But we also know that political reputations and careers are currently at stake because of that invasion, and that, in consequence, more than the truth is at play in the fierce arguments now raging about how and whether the USA and UK should have invaded Iraq without a clear international mandate. In fact, the heat of the exchanges in the immediate wake of the war has been so intense as to make the separation of fact from fiction extraordinarily difficult to achieve by anyone entering the fray without prior and independent evidence on who exactly said what, when and with what veracity. It is that prior evidence that we now intend to gather here.

Justifications for the Invasion

In general, four justifications were given for the invasion of Iraq.

The war on terrorism

When Iraq first entered the international equation that led eventually to its invasion, it did so as the target of an argument on terrorism

and the need to fight it. In moving against Iraq, the USA (and to a
degree, the UK) Government claimed to be participating in the 'first
war of the twenty-first century – the war against terrorism'. 'Every
nation', Tony Blair told the House of Commons in November 2002,
now faces 'the menace of international terrorism and weapons of
mass destruction'; every nation now faces a new kind of threat from
real and invisible enemies: from fanatics and from the states that
support them. 'They won't go more lightly on us', he said, 'if we are
less outspoken in our condemnation of them', for 'extremism has just
taken a new form for the twenty-first century.'[2] What happened on
9/11 was an unannounced and premeditated attack. It was not conventional warfare, with armies facing each other in open combat, but
– so the argument ran – it was war nonetheless. For although the
events of 9/11 were the product of non-state violence, this was a new
form of violence that could be orchestrated only from within safe
havens provided by particular states. And because it could only be so
orchestrated, the military response to it – as George Bush made clear
in the post-9/11 address to Congress that Tony Blair witnessed at
first hand – had necessarily and legitimately to be directed *both* at the
direct perpetrators of the violence *and* at the states that harboured
them.

As we have seen, it was as such a state – as a 'state harbouring
terrorists' – that the regime of Saddam Hussein in Iraq first entered
the post-9/11 scenario as laid out in Washington and then in London. Saddam Hussein was reintroduced to the US people with increasing frequency after the fall of Kabul as a threat to their national
security. He was reintroduced as part of the Administration's response to the events of 9/11, because of his supposed links to, and
support of, the Islamic radicals responsible for the attacks on the
World Trade Center and the Pentagon. The removal of Hussein from
power was proffered initially, that is, both in Washington and in
London, as a way of undermining the threat posed to US interests
and homeland security by the terrorist wing of radical Islam. This
claim was made at the beginning of the campaign against Iraq. It was
made in the middle.[3] It was also made at the end. So George Bush, in
declaring 'major combat operations' over, told the world from the
deck of the *USS Abraham Lincoln*:

> [T]he Battle of Baghdad is one victory in a war on terror that began on
> 11 September 2001, and still goes on. . . . We have removed an ally of
> al-Qaeda, and cut off a source of terrorist funding. And this much is
> certain. No terrorist network will gain weapons of mass destruction
> from the Iraqi regime, because that regime is no more.[4]

The key argument here was one of linkage; and as we saw in chapter 4, that linkage could be asserted as either 'direct' or 'indirect' in kind. In fact, over time and as the evidence of *direct* linkage between Iraq and al-Qaeda proved illusive, it was the *indirect* connections, and the *possibilities of direct ones*, that were increasingly cited in both London and Washington as necessitating unilateral and speedy action. The Bush Administration never entirely abandoned the direct linkage claim. Colin Powell made it before the UN as late as 5 February 2003, and George Bush repeated it in a major speech on 27 February. 'This same tyrant', he told the American Enterprise Institute, 'has close ties to terrorist organizations' (the direct link), and 'could supply them with the terrible means to strike this country' (the indirect one).[5] And when Deputy Defense Secretary Wolfowitz was challenged on the weakness of that claim, in relation specifically to the attacks on 9/11, he persisted in its defence by using the 'tip of an iceberg' strategy for extrapolating large conclusions from small amounts of evidence. Thus:

> QUESTION Mr Wolfowitz, you constantly infer a connection between Saddam Hussein and terrorism and Iraq and September 11th, and yet you provide no evidence. Is that because there is no evidence?
>
> WOLFOWITZ Well, first of all I haven't constantly inferred anything of the kind you say. But the fact is that there are connections. If you go back, for example, and read George Tenet's unclassified letter to the Senate Intelligence Committee, about two months ago, which got a lot of attention. . . . There's a great deal of detail in there that summarizes on an unclassified basis what our intelligence people have concluded to date. Iraqi connections to al-Qaeda, and of course, we know about many other Iraqi connections to terrorists of different kinds including widely advertised bounties that they provide to the families of suicide bombers. It's a long record, some of it out in the open. But it's the nature of state support for terrorism that a great deal of it is concealed. One sort of sees a tip of an iceberg, but that tip has been described, and I suggest you go back and read the Tenet letter if you want a summary.[6]

The UK's Foreign Secretary said this on the eve of the invasion itself:

> After the initial shock and horror provoked by the terrorist attacks of 11 September, one of my first thoughts was that there were – and are – no limits to the terrorists' appetite for slaughter. If they can lay their hands on weapons of mass destruction they will use them. The most likely source of materials and know-how are those rogue regimes that

show total disregard for the rule of law, and share the terrorists' hatred of our values. Some will suggest that this is overly alarmist, that Saddam is far too concerned with self-preservation ever to pass weapons of mass destruction to terrorist groups. Personally, I am not prepared to make any assumptions about the motivations of this dictator. Who would have predicated his ruinous war of aggression against Iran, or his invasion of Kuwait? In 1990, who knew that Saddam was within three years of his ultimate ambition, a nuclear weapon? We cannot afford to assume that we can second-guess his next move. Given Saddam Hussein's longstanding support for terrorist causes, does anyone seriously expect us to rule out the terrifying possibility that his poisons and diseases will find their way into the hands of al-Qaeda and its sympathizers. After all, his regime has sheltered the notorious Palestinian terrorist, Abu Nidal, for many years.[7]

In light of the difficulties that both Washington and London experienced later in demonstrating linkages between the Iraqi regime and al-Qaeda, it should never be forgotten that the claim that 'the liberation of Iraq is a crucial advance in the campaign against terror'[8] was the first main reason given for the refocusing of the attention of the world from Kabul to Baghdad after the USA and UK succeeded in achieving regime change in Afghanistan. It is true that, as those difficulties intensified, other justifications for military intervention moved centre-stage; but the anti-terrorism claim never entirely vanished. Indeed, it is also the case that anti-terrorism tended to resurface as the main justification for military intervention whenever the evidence necessary to sustain those other justifications also proved difficult to obtain; and of course it left a huge legacy in the American mind. As late as September 2003, opinion polls were still reporting that a staggering 70 per cent of the US population remained convinced that Saddam Hussein was directly involved in the planning of the attacks on 9/11, when actually, as we know, he was not.[9]

Unregulated weapons of mass destruction

Very quickly in the build-up of the public case against the Baghdad regime, however, the basis on which Iraq was said to constitute a clear and present danger to the United States, and to the rest of the 'civilized world', began to change. As we have seen, after George Bush's 2002 State of the Union Address, the regime of Saddam Hussein found itself labelled as one of three states (Iran and North Korea being the others) that constituted a more general 'axis of evil'. Through that labelling, Iraq's threat to US homeland security via its supposed support of Islamic terrorism was incrementally subsumed into a new danger that the regime in Baghdad was said to pose: that of a general threat to US and western interests in the Arab region – to oil interests in the Gulf states, and to political interests in the security of the state of Israel – rooted in Baghdad's possession of weapons of mass destruction.

The argument here had both a general and an Iraqi dimension. In general, as the advocates of the new theory of pre-emptive retaliation repeatedly argued, defence against this upsurge of terrorism had to be designed against the background of the existence for the first time of small weapons with big impacts. Those charged with national security now had a novel problem with which to deal. They had to address how to cope with weapons that are small in size and visibility but large in their capacity indiscriminately to kill. Or rather, they had to cope with the possibility of the use of such weapons by a new set of global players. For the major powers had long had such 'weapons of mass destruction' – nuclear, chemical and biological – the latter two categories of which at least, because they are small yet deadly, are easy to conceal and require relatively little formal infrastructure to build and to deploy. The problem now, however, is that their possession and use might proliferate. It is not just that the western democracies face real and invisible enemies. It is also that those enemies have the potential to acquire real and invisible weapons; such that even if Iraq is not such an enemy, it might well be a source of such weapons for those who are.

In this way, to the problems supposedly posed to western interests by links between Baghdad and al-Qaeda were then added the dangers posed to the region by Saddam Hussein's possession of weapons of mass destruction. The regime in Iraq was said to be a danger to regional and global stability because of its possession of a set of biological and chemical weapons unaccounted for by the UN inspectors when they left in 1998, and because of its pursuit of a nuclear weapons capability: a capability, we were now told, that it was likely to possess within probably two years and certainly five. The regime was also said to be such a danger because of its refusal to cooperate with the UN inspectorate sent into Iraq under the agreement that ended the first Gulf War, an inspectorate charged with the monitoring and destruction of precisely these sets of weapons. As we have seen, throughout 2002 the Bush Administration regularly reported to the world that the Iraqi government was in possession of a chemical and biological arsenal, that it was actively developing its own nuclear capacity and that it would soon have its own nuclear weapons; and that these actual and potential weapons far exceeded any capacity that Iraq required for its own self-defence. Throughout 2002, and right through to the invasion itself, the UK Government then regularly replicated those reports. Jack Straw, for example, in February 2003, said:

> Saddam Hussein's regime typifies these threats. He has challenged the international order for over a decade. Weapons of mass destruction have been a central pillar of Saddam's dictatorship since the 1980s. He has amassed poisons and viruses both to suppress his own people and to threaten his neighbours. He has relentlessly pursued his ultimate ambition, the acquisition of a nuclear weapons capability, in flagrant disregard of Security Council Resolutions and Iraq's obligations as a non-nuclear weapon state under the non-proliferation treaty. His pursuit of these weapons has lain at the heart of the UN's stand-off with Iraq for the past 12 years.[10]

Rogue states and regime change

It was this 'weapons of mass destruction argument' that then triggered the third of the direct justificatory theses used later to justify invasion. The possession of such weapons by Saddam Hussein's regime, we were told, indicated a propensity on the part of the Iraqis to invade neighbouring states, and implied the continued commitment of the Iraqi Government to some undeclared desire for regional hegemony of the kind that had sent their forces into Kuwait in 1990. We also began to hear a drumbeat of concern about the use of such weapons by the regime internally, against Kurdish resistance in the early 1980s, particularly the dropping of chemical weapons on the northern Kurdish village of Halabja in March 1988, which killed at least 5,000 people and injured another 10,000. This was evidence, we were told, that was indicative of the unique degree to which the Iraqi regime was willing to combine external aggression with internal repression of a particularly venal kind. Jack Straw spoke of the 'only government in the world to have fired missiles at five of its neighbours, invaded two of them, and gassed its own people':[11]

> We . . . have to differentiate between the threat posed by Iraq and other would-be proliferators. No other country shares Iraq's history of deploying chemical weapons in a war of aggression against a neighbour, or against innocent civilians as part of a genocidal campaign. It is this deadly combination of capability and intent which makes Saddam uniquely dangerous.[12]

Throughout 2002, the vilification of Saddam Hussein by the Bush Administration went on apace. Again and again, he was likened to

Hitler; and those opposed to immediate military action against him were repeatedly reminded of the bankruptcy of appeasement in the 1930s. It was by this 1930s route that what had begun late in 2001 as an argument about weakening terrorist networks, and denying them lethal weaponry, then gathered a further justificatory strand, and one whose importance would grow over time: namely that of democratization imposed from outside. The governing parallel moved from Afghanistan in 2001 to Germany in 1945, and the impending invasion was repackaged as an act of liberation. Indeed, the US military actually retitled their war plan 'Operation Iraqi Freedom'; and Tony Blair told the BBC World Service that the attack on Iraq 'was genuinely a war, not of conquest, but of liberation'.[13] It must be noted, however, that, prior to the invasion, the weight of the parallel with the Nazis was on Hussein's and Hitler's shared propensity for the conquering of neighbouring states, rather than on their similarly structured regimes of terror; and it needs to be remembered too that, again prior to the invasion, the main focus in the justificatory case remained heavily on the dangers of terrorism and weapons of mass destruction, rather than on breaches of human rights by the Iraqi regime. Tony Blair was quite explicit on this when praising the outcome of the NATO summit held in Prague in November 2002, a summit whose resulting communiqué made, in his view,

> a remarkable statement of defiance ... [linking] clearly and rightly terrorism and weapons of mass destruction. The threat from weapons of mass destruction in the hands of rogue unstable states is not part of some different danger. It too represents savage indifference to human life. It too crosses national boundaries without discrimination. It too can't be negotiated with or appeased, only defeated utterly.[14]

Tony Blair was also quite explicit through the early months of 2003 that, despicable as the Iraqi regime was, the UK Government was prepared to see it remain in existence if it was willing fully to comply with a rigorous programme of UN-led weapons inspection[15] (the Bush Administration, we must remember, was not so explicit). But nonetheless, and by the time the troops actually went in to Iraq on 21 March 2003, the issue of democratization was there, playing a subordinate role in the justificatory structure surrounding their invasion. It was there, available to move onto the centre of the justificatory stage once the achievement of regime change in Baghdad failed to produce the much-vaunted weapons of mass destruction.

Global governance

To this linked set of arguments, one other central body of assertions was added in the months leading up to the invasion: namely, that a slower and more incremental internationally orchestrated containment of this particularly dangerous and unpleasant regime was no longer viable. Iraq, we were told repeatedly, stood 'in material breach' of a string of UN Security Council resolutions, not least 1441 itself. The American popular media visited again the lost opportunity of the first Gulf War, the disastrous failure of the first Bush Administration to support the anti-Hussein risings in the north and the south of Iraq that followed, and the sorry saga of the UN inspectorate's struggles and withdrawal from Iraq as the Baghdad regime regained its composure and self-confidence in the 1990s. True, the second Bush Administration was persuaded to take the UN route again, pushed reluctantly down that road by pressure from 'doves' within the Administration and from its UK ally; and, as we know, UNSCR 1441 did send the UN inspectors back into Iraq in pursuit of the regime's lethal and hidden arsenals, and sent them back with a significantly expanded capacity to do their work. But the timescale set by the Bush Administration for the completion of the renewed inspection, and the evidence required by Washington to demonstrate full Iraqi compliance with it in the wake of twelve years of Iraqi procrastination, were from the outset much tighter than what was required by other Security Council members, even including at times, it should be noted, the UK itself. The Administration's argument here was that the Iraqi regime was particularly gifted at misleading inspectors, that delay only increased the likelihood of the proliferation of lethal weaponry to terrorists, and that Iraqi compliance was directly proportional to the threat of external military force. In the end, the justification for the timing of the invasion and its deployment without a second UN resolution of support turned on this issue more than on any other. It turned on the claim that UNSCR 1441 was enough to legitimate the use of military force if evidence of Iraqi non-compliance was demonstrated. It turned on the claim that Iraq under the leadership of Saddam Hussein constituted a real and present danger to regional stability, to US interests and to the successful pursuit of the war on terrorism; and that because it did, the world could not afford to wait more than the twelve years it had waited already. It could not even afford to wait the four months that Hans Blix, the chief UN inspector, claimed was necessary for the completion of his mission. So at least we were told.

Was the War Justified?

Some of the justificatory arguments for this invasion have real force; and this is not to be wondered at. For contrary to the more simplistic responses that sometimes come from people opposed to exercises of this kind, what we face here is not a straightforward matter of the informed against the stupid, with the stupid unfortunately being currently in charge of the lunatic asylum. On the contrary, two of the central justificatory strands in the arguments for this war are undeniably true; and their force must be recognized by those of us who remain convinced that a unilateral military invasion of Iraq was an inappropriate response to them. It is undeniably true that the regime of Saddam Hussein was a particularly repressive one, whose removal would free the Iraqi people from 'decades and decades of torture and oppression'.[16] And 9/11 did happen. The United States was attacked by forces claiming to speak for radical Islam; and because it was, and because the threat of further attacks remains in place, US foreign policy does indeed have to address the threat posed by radical Islamic terrorist groups as one of its core concerns.

The evidence on the horrendous character of the Hussein regime, as distinct from the evidence on its impending military adventurism, is plentiful and unambiguous, and was readily so long before US and UK troops entered Iraq. In fact, the US State Department issued its annual global review of human rights only days before the invasion began, and quite properly ranked Iraq in its top two or three regimes of terror. That review reported a horrendous string of human rights abuses in the Iraqi case: such things as arbitrary arrest, summary executions, and the systematic use of torture, beatings and rape against opponents and their families.[17] Moreover, the attacks on the World Trade Center and Pentagon on 9/11 did place at the core of the foreign policy agenda of all the western democracies the issue of how best to respond to non-state-generated violence, and how to do so in a context in which that violence would come unannounced. The events of 9/11 did, and do, present western defence experts with the issue of how best to prevent such violence in an age of readily available technologies of mass destruction. And it is germane to the proper resolution of this new policy dilemma to recognize that, in a post-Cold War world, the proliferation of those weaponries is now much harder to contain. How best to govern the world, in order to avoid nuclear holocaust and the proliferation of chemical and biological weapons, is a pressing contemporary issue: as too is the question of how best to reset political structures in the Middle East to establish peace, stability and social justice in that region. It is true that issues such as these are in no sense new; but it is also true that what *is* new is the changed context in which they have now to be addressed.

So there can be no legitimate grievance against those who place such items of concern at the forefront of the modern foreign policy debate. We can and should, of course, point out that many other key elements of global concern – from poverty to environmental degradation – do not receive as focused an attention in Washington (or even in truth in London) as do questions of terrorism and war. Fighting over the relative priority of the 'soft' threats of poverty, disease and environmental devastation against the 'hard' threats of terrorism and war is legitimate and necessary. But what is more legitimate and important right now is the struggle against the way in which Washington and London have currently decided to seek the resolution of their own narrower agenda. For though the indirect arguments used to justify the military intervention in Iraq do have a certain force, what does *not* have any force at all is the claim that these legitimate defence concerns are best answered, even in the short term, by unilateral military intervention of the kind undertaken by the USA and the UK in Iraq. It is true that the world is a more dangerous place for US and UK citizens in the wake of 9/11. It is not true that the world has been made safer for them again by externally imposed and unilaterally initiated regime change in Baghdad.

On the contrary, there is every justification for the counter-view: that invading Iraq in this unilateral way was exactly the *wrong* response to the sets of concerns released by the attack on the World Trade Center and the growing evidence of the internally repressive nature of the Iraqi regime. If winning the war on terrorism was the real goal, invading Iraq in this fashion has actually made achieving that goal even harder. If reducing the proliferation and use of weapons of mass destruction was the real aim, invading Iraq in this fashion took the action away from the main sources of this new danger. If spreading democracy in the Middle East was the real aim, externally imposed regime change in Baghdad was the least likely way of guaranteeing long-term success. And if reducing the threat posed by radical Islam to US and UK homeland security was the aim, no policy could have been invented that was less likely to succeed n the long term than that of using western troops to depose an Arab dictator.

The counter-arguments run as follows.

The link with terrorism

The war cannot be legitimated by the scale and character of any pre-war linkage between the Hussein regime and the terrorist organizations of radical Islam. <u>On the contrary, the war stood fair to strengthen</u> <u>those linkages, so making its justification self-fulfilling</u>.[18] It certainly moved Saddam Hussein from villain to hero among large sections of the Arab world, particularly among the young unemployed men of the Arab street.

The linkage asserted, in justification of military intervention, between the Iraqi regime and al-Qaeda was always an extraordinarily thin one. There is just no evidence that the events of 9/11 were directly connected to the Iraqi regime at all, or that al-Qaeda was in receipt of any significant quantity of Iraqi aid or support. On the contrary, prior to the invasion, the Iraqi regime was a prime example of the kind of corrupt secular regime that al-Qaeda wished to see replaced by a fundamentalist Islamic one. It is worth remembering in this regard that the early pronouncements of the radical Islamists who later came together to form al-Qaeda were not directed at the United States. That came later, mainly in the wake of the first Gulf War. The initial targets of the organizations and radical Islamic thinkers who are now linked in various ways to al-Qaeda were internal and regional. Their targets were Arab leaders whom they considered 'heretical': particularly secular nationalists and Baathist leaders and regimes in the Arab world, including Saddam Hussein himself. Indeed, bin Laden is on record as offering his mujadin fighters for the protection of Saudi Arabia against Iraq in the wake of the Iraqi invasion of Kuwait in 1990. So it is hardly surprising, in the light of this history of antagonism between secular modernizers and religious fundamentalists, that Colin Powell, in addressing the UN, was unable to establish other than the most vestigial direct links between Baghdad and radical Islamic terrorist groups; and that the UK Government, when issuing its dossier against Saddam Hussein, never even tried to establish those links at all.[19]

In fact, all the evidence we have suggests that the pre-invasion, pre-9/11 Iraqi regime was neither sympathetic to, nor interested in, al-Qaeda or other radical Islamic groups and movements;[20] and that, in consequence, if the Bush Administration had really wanted to go sequentially after the countries supporting radical Islam in the wake of the fall of the Taliban, then its logical next target should have been the Saudis. <u>For it is from Saudi Arabia that fundamentalist</u> <u>Islam receives its greatest state and private funding, and it is in Saudi</u> <u>Arabia that fundamentalist Islam enjoys its largest mass following</u>. It is in the Saudi version of Islam that fundamentalism flourishes; and it is in the Wahhabi schools across the Middle East, financed by the Saudis, that al-Qaeda and similar radical Islamic organizations find willing recruits.[21] Iraq was not even the next in line here after Saudi

Arabia in the list of states breeding terrorism: arguably that would have been Pakistan. Yet the Saudis, of course, were not targeted by the US Administration or the UK Government, any more than was Pakistan, because for decades the Saudi royal family has been a main prop for the western democracies in the oil fields and oil markets of a region that is so vital to western economic success; and because Pakistan was a newly won ally in the fight against the Taliban. As far as US and UK governments were concerned, oil interests seemed to prevail over terrorism concerns in the heartland of Islamic fundamentalism, but not, it would seem, in the case of the more moderately Islamic Iraq. The question we have to ask is 'why?'

Weapons of mass destruction

The question is all the more pressing because it is not clear from the evidence of the Iraqis' relative non-involvement with Islamic fundamentalism that Saddam Hussein's regime did represent a 'real and present' danger to the United States.[22] It is not even clear that it did still possess weapons of mass destruction; or that, if it did, it was planning in the immediate future either to use them to alter the local power-balance and/or to attack the United States or its allies (especially Israel), or to release them to any terrorist networks. It was not even obvious that if Iraq was part of an 'axis of evil' with North Korea and Iran – which was in any case a very strange claim to make, given the history of animosity between Iraq and Iran under Saddam Hussein – it was potentially the most lethal member of it. We only have to compare the absence of an immediate Iraqi nuclear capacity with the possession of such a capacity in North Korea and Iran to see the strangeness of the claim.[23] Certainly, major governments elsewhere in the advanced capitalist world were not persuaded that Iraq constituted the main and immediate danger to regional and global peace, as London and Washington insisted it to be; and the Bush/Blair team never made an adequate public defence of this critical assertion.

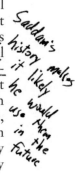

Saddam's history makes it likely he would use them in the future

Of course, prior to the invasion of Iraq there may have been security reasons for the Bush/Blair hesitancy – something to do with protecting sources of intelligence that stopped them piling up the evidence of the Iraqi threat in public – but clearly they failed to make the 'Iraq is an immediate threat' case convincingly in private either, even to the heads of governments of France, Germany, Russia or China. It seems to stretch credulity to its breaking point to believe that Bush and Blair really did make a powerful private case about the Iraqi threat, only for *all* those governments to put their immediate economic interests before the needs of long-term global security. Even if the French were mischievous here – and that has never been proved, just asserted – the others had no such incentive to be uncooperative. On the contrary, the Russians in particular have a powerful interest in joint US/Russian moves against Islamic fundamentalism – in Chechnya as well as in the Middle East – and yet the Russian President Putin was just as initially critical of Bush as the French President Chirac, and just as subsequently unrepentant.

For though it was not publicly known prior to the invasion (it certainly became quickly known after the invasion), it is now clear that the Bush Administration deliberately and 'grossly manipulated intelligence about those weapons of mass destruction in the run up to the Iraq war'.[24] In fact, Paul Wolfowitz went on record as early as 30 May 2003 as saying that 'the Bush Administration focused on alleged weapons of mass destruction as the primary justification for toppling Saddam Hussein by force because it was politically convenient . . . because it was the one reason everyone could agree on'.[25] Indeed, if the *New York Times* is to be believed, the resulting 'outrage among the intelligence professionals' at this misuse of their preliminary data was 'so widespread that they formed a group, Veteran Intelligence Professionals for Sanity, that wrote to President Bush . . . to protest what it called a policy and intelligence fiasco of monumental proportions'.[26] That fiasco could be obscured prior to the invasion of Iraq, but it proved progressively more difficult to obscure when the military phase of the Iraqi invasion was over. For what the invasion did, of course, was to provide the occupying powers with a clear opportunity to generate the evidence that could then justify their prior claim about the existence of weapons of mass destruction in Iraq. That opportunity existed both during the war (if any such weapons were used against the invading forces) or after it (if any such weapons were left lying around). But in the event, and as a string of public inquiries have subsequently shown, no such evidence has been (or apparently will be) forthcoming, since such weapons were not used by the Iraqis, nor were any immediately found by the military forces that defeated them. There was and is *no smoking gun*; and because there is not, those who had justified the invasion on these grounds now find themselves with an enormous amount of justifying of their own to do.

Thus far at least, in the immediate wake of the war, several escape routes have been opened up for that purpose. None of these justificatory escape routes, however, has proved to be particularly credible.

The first of these escape routes, briefly mentioned from Washington in the early post-invasion period, was a *dispersal and self-destruction* argument: that weapons of mass destruction could not initially be found by US and UK forces on the ground in Iraq because somehow Saddam Hussein's people had either destroyed these weapons or spread them around. Either they had been destroyed before the fighting began;[27] or they had gone across the border into Syria, exchanged for night-vision goggles or the like; or they had been distributed to terrorist groups and so smuggled out of Iraq. But these arguments beggar belief. Here was a regime fighting for its life, against a military force demanding its unconditional surrender and doing its best to assassinate its leading figures, and yet those leading figures were supposed to have chosen to give their best weapons away at their moment of greatest need, preferring to disperse them rather than use them in self-defence. It is significant in this regard that the 'evil monster' of this pantomime – 'Chemical Ali' – was reportedly based in Basra: and yet Basra fell to UK forces after a prolonged siege in which no chemical or biological weapons were used against UK forces. What then are we to believe? That the regime lost its nerve, or that it had no such weapons in the first place? For our part, we stand with Polly Toynbee: 'Saddam's non-use of the weapons even in the death throes of his regime was conclusive proof that he had none he could use.'[28]

Maybe the thought that weapons of mass destruction did not exist in any volume in Iraq prior to the invasion did creep into the minds of the very highest echelons of the Bush Administration early in the occupation phase of the US/UK invasion; for by the first week of May 2003 journalists were being briefed, off the record, that dispersal of another kind had occurred. To quote the *New York Times*:

> Senior aides, in interviews in recent days, [have] begun to back away from their prewar claims that Mr. Hussein had an arsenal that was loaded and ready to fire. They now contend that he developed what they call a 'just in time' production strategy for his weapons, hiding chemical precursors that could quickly be loaded into empty artillery shells or short-range missiles.[29]

In seeking to counter that particular dispersal escape route – since the US military could no more find a just-in-time military-industrial complex in Iraq than they could find huge stores of chemical and biological weapons – George Bush simply cautioned that it would take time to find the weapons because Saddam Hussein's regime had spent so many years hiding them. 'We'll find them', he said.[30] In other words, he used the second escape route that rapidly developed for those arguing the 'invade because of weapons of mass destruction' case: the argument of *wait and see*.

This was Tony Blair's line daily in the wake of the invasion: that the doubters would eventually have to eat their words, since intelligence sources had convinced him that weapons of mass destruction were in the possession of the Iraqi regime: weapons which, given time, US/UK investigating teams would uncover. As he put it when challenged on day 71 of the coalition occupation of Iraq about the continuing absence of the discovery of any weapons, and about the possible 'doctoring' of the dossier on Iraq issued by the UK Government prior to the war:

> You have just got to have a little bit of patience. I have absolutely no doubt at all when we produce the further evidence, that evidence will be found and I have absolutely no doubt it exists because Saddam's history of weapons of mass destruction is not some invention of the British security forces.[31]

To this the response must be threefold. At the very best, it suggests a double standard: the coalition forces now demanding that we show patience when it was precisely patience that they failed to show with Hans Blix, when he couldn't find the weapons either.[32] Moreover, if such weapons were there, awaiting discovery, why was the Bush Administration so reluctant to allow the UN inspectorate back in to find them? And even if that reluctance was a product more of presidential pique than of fear of non-discovery, it still remains the case that their inability immediately to find weapons of mass destruction totally obliterates the force of the claim, made repeatedly by both Washington and London prior to the invasion, that time here was of the essence. If these weapons were so obscure in location and limited in volume that they could remain undetected even when the UK and USA controlled Iraq, how are we to believe that, prior to the invasion, their extensive use or dissemination was daily imminent?

Since this invasion cannot therefore be properly justified either as a part of the war on terrorism or because of the imminent danger of the Iraqi deployment of weapons of mass destruction, on what grounds can it then be justified? Certainly not, without heavy qualification, on the two other grounds regularly deployed for this purpose.

The liberation and democratization of a rogue state

This is now the predominant official line, of course, that, from the outset, the invasion of Iraq by coalition forces was designed as a war of liberation, whose prime purpose was to set the Iraqi people free from a hideous regime and to trigger by example an extensive democratization process in the Arab world. The UK Government in particular lays great store by this claim, challenging its critics to deny that the world is a better place with Hussein gone. How can progressive people oppose an invasion, we are asked, with such a noble purpose and such a progressive outcome?

To which the response must be that the disagreement here is not about ends but about means. It is also about the centrality of this particular end to the invasion planning of the Bush Administration; and (as we will demonstrate in chapter 8) it is also about the use and abuse of the doctrine of humanitarian intervention, and the dangerous consequences of using human rights as a cover for a more complex mix of motives.

What is not in dispute here is the desire to see the replacement of dictatorial regimes by democratic ones. Who could reasonably oppose that? What is in dispute, however, is how democratization is to be triggered and by whom. That is *the* general issue to which we will return in chapter 8. But first we have to question, in the specifics of the Iraqi case, the degree to which the commitment to liberation and democratization in this invasion was and is either genuine or central. It may be both to Tony Blair; but was it, and is it, to George Bush? We doubt it; and because we do, we sense that the high moral tone (and ambition) of the UK project in Iraq has been wedded to, and suborned by, a US project in which democratization is far more fig-leaf than substance.

There is one important piece of evidence that plays to the democratization case: and that is the manner in which the US and UK military conducted themselves during the invasion itself. Military commanders were clearly keen to limit the scale of death and destruction: certainly the scale of damage imposed on the civilian population, but also, to a lesser degree, that imposed on regular units of the Iraqi army as well. The Iraqi death toll after 20 March was very high, and, to their shame, remains both uncounted and unreported by the bulk of the western press. But even so, it would appear that in general the US and UK military commanders applied most of their deadly force to Baathist officials and their irregular militias. The air war was more indiscriminate in its pattern of slaughter; but even then clear efforts were made to limit what is often euphemistically labelled 'collateral damage'; and certainly, once the fighting was over, coalition forces moved quickly to play a reconstruction role, to generate an interim Iraqi administration and to plan their own departure. All of which suggests that, once under way, the invasion of Iraq did attract to itself the task of democratizing the political system there – or certainly, of generating a civil society that was not inherently anti-western. But that, unfortunately, is not the key issue. The key issue is whether democratization was a major triggering motive for invasion or just one picked up along the way; and to that question there is much counter-evidence in the Bush case, and in the history of US administrations past and present, that needs to be taken into account.

Certainly, the post-1945 record of the USA on the question of liberation and democracy is very patchy. US administrations of both parties have in times past supported, and occasionally actively orchestrated, the actual *removal* of democratically elected regimes, and have quite regularly supported and armed dictators and tyrants (including, throughout the 1980s, Saddam Hussein himself). The list of examples of anti-democratic moves by previous US Administrations would certainly have to include Guatemala in 1954, Brazil in 1964, Chile in 1973, Argentina in 1976 and Nicaragua in the early 1980s. And 11 September is, after all, a key date in Chilean history too. It was the date in 1973 when a US-backed military coup overthrew the democratically elected government of Salvador Allende, at the immediate cost of more than 3,000 lives. Of course, there is no overriding reason why George W. Bush's Administration should be tarred with those brushes from administrations long gone: no reason, that is, except that the current US Ambassador to the United Nations was actually Ambassador in Managua when Ronald Reagan's Administration was giving covert help to the Contras in Nicaragua. John Negroponte was quite a choice for George W. Bush to make as UN Ambassador if global democratization was, from the outset of his election, the overriding policy goal![33]

It needs to be remembered too that, although the repressive nature of the regime in Baghdad has only recently become a matter of general public record, it was in fact well known in policy-making circles in both the USA and the UK from the very beginning of Saddam Hussein's rule. Yet it took more than twenty years for his regime's methods to become so morally intolerable that unilateral military action was deemed suddenly to be imperative.[34] As Ann Feltham from the Campaign Against Arms Trade noted *before* the invasion took place, although she and others had campaigned against arms sales to Iraq in the 1980s because of the regime's record on human rights, Tony Blair and Jack Straw did not give that campaign their support.[35] As Rivers Pitt has put it so well:

> We must come to a disturbing conclusion, based on the facts at hand. Saddam Hussein is a monster, by any definition, but he is our monster. He is as much an American creation as Coca-Cola and the Oldsmobile. Our government supported his regime during his war

typical rhetoric

with Iran, a war in which he used chemical weapons on the battlefield with our full knowledge, with our arms, money and military intelligence. The United States did not remove him during the Gulf War and in fact thwarted attempts by Iraqi insurgents – inspired to act by our rhetoric – to overthrow his regime.[36]

Indeed, there is a cruel irony in the way that this operation to unseat Saddam Hussein was overseen by the current US Secretary of Defense, given that he was the first major figure in the Republican Establishment actually to visit Baghdad in the immediate aftermath of the Iraqi use of chemical weapons in 1983.[37] Clearly, moral outrage gestated only very slowly in senior Republican circles in the 1980s and 1990s, and then only in very partial ways. For although the Bush Administration suddenly became so keen to democratize Iraq that democratization was trotted out as a justification for war, we heard very little about a roadmap to democratize US allies in the Middle East, such as Saudi Arabia or Egypt, until some seven months after the war began – and more than two years after elements of the Saudi regime were linked to 9/11 far more convincingly than Saddam Hussein ever was.

Nor, if first signs are any guide, was there much of a roadmap in Washington ahead of the invasion on how exactly to democratize Iraq itself after it had been 'liberated'. Certainly there was nothing planned ahead of time with the precision and detail of the planning that went into the military side of this 'democratic liberation'. In fact, the only groups seemingly well prepared to govern Iraq in the wake of Saddam Hussein are the very clerical forces which, two decades earlier in Iran, turned a popular revolution there into a repressive 'theocratic democracy' antagonistic to the West. This can hardly have been the outcome that US planners had in mind. And even in Afghanistan, which is further along this road of democratization under coalition protection than is Iraq, the nation-building process is staggering from crisis to crisis, with warlordism still intact and the rights of women still far from guaranteed. So if the US is on some global or regional drive to democracy, it is a drive that is patchy and self-serving at best, and self-defeating at worst. Maybe the UK can guarantee democracy in Basra: but it stretches belief to hold to the view that the democratization of the rest of Iraq was actually the prime motive for the Bush Administration, rather than simply one of its prime legitimating covers. And because it does stretch belief, it must leave a huge question-mark over the relevance and function of the UK Government's continued assertion of moral purpose here. In a world influenced by Richard Perle, who is the bigger fool: us or Tony Blair?

New forms of global governance

So was this invasion rather a matter of implementing UN resolutions by a US and UK military force that had a clear UN mandate, one triggered into action because of an impasse in global governance created by an unholy alliance between Hussein chicanery and French intransigence? For this is the other legitimating argument commonly deployed to replace the waning one of 'weapons of mass destruction': namely, that the USA and UK were forced to act unilaterally because the Security Council was blocked by French-led intransigence, and because Saddam Hussein was leading the UN inspectors on his usual procrastinating dance, as he had done for twelve years past. Did the USA and UK go into Iraq to impose the UN's rule of law, an imposition that was long overdue, and whose absence through the 1990s had corroded the UN's credibility and standing?

Again, the answer has to be 'No'. As we saw, the invasion occurred without a second resolution ordering military action, against the background of the first resolution (1441), which did not do so, and which passed the UN Security Council in November 2002 only because, for the majority of countries signing it, it was seen *not* to authorize the use of force. The desperate, and in the end, futile search for a second resolution by the USA (and particularly the UK) only made sense if 1441 was generally recognized not to be sufficient justification for military action; and yet military action was taken even so, and the UN was sidelined in the process. The US and UK Governments can now say that they want the UN to play a major role in the reconstruction of Iraq – though in fact it is the UK Government alone that is saying that with any regularity – but neither government can credibly deny that, by their actions, they both seriously undermined the standing of the UN and seriously weakened the emerging systems of international law.

This, after all, was the major reason given by Robin Cook for his resignation from the Blair Cabinet on the eve of the invasion: that unilateral military action by the USA and UK acting in concert would undermine the credibility of international institutions in whose strengthening the UK had a clear national interest. As he wrote at the time:

> If we believe in an international community based on binding rules and institutions, we cannot simply set them aside when they produce results that are inconvenient to us. I cannot defend a war with neither international agreement nor domestic support. I applaud the determined

efforts . . . to secure a second resolution. Now that those attempts have ended in failure, we cannot pretend that getting a second resolution was of no importance. . . . The harsh reality is that Britain is being asked to embark on a war without agreement in any of the international bodies of which we are a leading member. Not NATO. Not the EU. And now not the Security Council. . . . Britain is not a superpower. Our interests are best protected, not by unilateral action, but by multilateral agreement and a world order governed by rules. Yet tonight the international partnerships most important to us are weakened. The European Union is divided. The Security Council is stalemated. These are heavy casualties of war without a single shot yet being fired.[38]

In fact the US/UK timetable and that of the UN were in tension throughout the build-up to the invasion. As we saw in chapter 3, George W. Bush was reluctant to go to the UN at all. Colin Powell alone persuaded him (at the now widely cited August 2002 briefing). The inspectors offered an alternative timetable, of only a few extra months, which Bush refused, thereby casting aside the international legitimacy that it would have given him. In truth, it is hard to tell quite what the US Administration would have lost by keeping their troops in the region unused for the period the inspectors required, and thus either forcing Hussein's hand or making it clear to the international community at large that the inspection regime had been given its full chance, and had failed. It is not exactly clear why Bush let himself be seen to be so visibly in a hurry, and in the process lose the legitimacy of UN support and undermine UN credibility. Was it because of a military timetable driven by the fear of the army degrading if it were kept too long at sea? Was it because of the window of opportunity fixed by weather? Was it because, having been so strident so early, neither Bush nor Blair could retreat without losing face, so strengthening both the Iraqi regime and al-Qaeda by pulling the troops back?[39] Or was it because sections of the Bush team actually wanted the fight? It is difficult to tell; but there is no doubt that the diplomatic route was not exhausted by the USA and the UK, no matter what they claim. It was terminated.

Nor can either Bush or Blair easily escape the claim of partiality: for in censuring Saddam Hussein for breaching UN resolutions, they conveniently failed to censure Israel with the same degree of vigour for an even longer track record of being in breach; and that double standard ate away at both the credibility of their claim to be acting under international law and the policy goal of undermining support for anti-American terrorism in the Middle East. Robin Cook was very clear on this in his resignation statement.

> I have heard it said that Iraq has had not months but twelve years in which to disarm, and our patience is exhausted. Yet it is over thirty years since resolution 242 called on Israel to withdraw from the occupied territories. We do not express the same impatience with the persistent refusal of Israel to comply.[40]

The Bush Administration could claim, and did, that it had a roadmap for a Palestinian state on hold until the Palestinian Authority had created leaders with whom it was prepared to deal – and under UK pressure, the Administration did in the end release that roadmap. But this was a classic example of too little, too late.[41] It could also be claimed that concentrating only on the issue of non-compliance with UN resolutions obscured crucial differences between the Israeli and Iraqi cases, and played to anti-Israeli sentiment by neglecting other cases of non-compliance. But the death toll in the second Intifada was just too large and too present in the television reporting of the Arab world for the US and UK claim to be liberators to have any credibility at all, even among very moderate Arab opinion.[42] On the contrary, the whole design of the invasion of Iraq actually ate away at the Middle East peace process in at least two crucial ways. By defining everything post-9/11 as a war on terrorism and by justifying US unilateral military action beyond its borders in terms of that war, the Bush Administration gave the green light to the Israeli Government to claim and do exactly the same. The 'war on terrorism' helped to destroy the peace process in Israel itself; and in the process of invading Iraq without general Arab support, the war strengthened the very forces – the Israeli and American Right, and radical Islam – that are most opposed to the peace process. Tony Blair and his ministers might privately feel that, by staying with Bush, they won the roadmap: this might indeed be, privately, one of their main justificatory claims. But the terms on which they chose to stay with the Bush Administration actually built higher and higher barriers to the successful achievement of the goal of the roadmap itself.

So this invasion does not stand, and cannot stand, as the latest example of the UK's involvement in a just war; and that is not simply our judgement. It is also the judgement of no less an international figure than former US President and winner of the 2002 Nobel Prize for Peace, Jimmy Carter, who had this to say about the war in Iraq even before it began:

> For a war to be just it must meet several clearly defined criteria. The war can be waged only as a last resort, with all nonviolent options exhausted. . . . The war's weapons must discriminate between combatants and non-combatants. . . . Its violence must be proportional to the

injury we suffered. . . . The attackers must have legitimate authority
sanctioned by the society they profess to represent . . . [and] the peace
it establishes must be a clear improvement over what exists. . . . As a
Christian and a president who was severely provoked by international
crises, I became thoroughly familiar with [these] principles, and it is
clear that a substantially unilateral attack on Iraq does not meet these
standards.[43]

Defending the War

Not surprisingly, therefore, in the end it turned out to be the case
that the only thing that was immediately destroyed by Iraq's weapons
of mass destruction was the credibility of the politicians who had
asserted their existence. As Vice-President Gore put it, the Bush Administration was guilty of:

> [allowing] false impressions to somehow make their way into the pub-
> lic's mind . . . that Saddam Hussein was involved in the September 11
> attacks and was actively supporting al-Qaeda; that Saddam's weapons
> of mass destruction were an imminent threat, and Iraq was on the verge
> of building nuclear weapons; that US troops would be welcomed with
> open arms, and there was little danger of continued casualties in a
> prolonged guerrilla war.[44]

None of that was true, of course; and so by the mid-summer of
2003 the US public, in spite of extraordinarily supine reporting of the
war by the bulk of the US media, was evenly split on this very issue:
with 48 per cent believing the accuracy of the President's claims and
47 per cent saying he had exaggerated them.[45] And by then the situation was no better in London. There, with a far more hostile press
and sceptical populace, Tony Blair went off on vacation conceding
that a serious lack of trust (because of exaggerated claims in relation
to Iraq) was still 'an issue we have to confront'.[46] Yet by then, that
confrontation had already been well over three months in the making
and had already developed its own recognizable pattern.

The least attractive part of that pattern was the ferocity with which,
on occasion, those who had advocated the war responded to criti-
cisms of how they had constructed their advocacy – not to mention
the speed with which key players tried to pass the buck from themselves to others as holes appeared in the claims they had made. The
clearest example of buck-passing occurred in Washington, as first
one official and then another was fingered as the source of the exaggerated claim about Iraq, uranium and Niger that appeared in the

2003 State of the Union Address.[47] The clearest case of ferocity of response occurred in London however, in the bitter, prolonged and no-holes-barred argument that developed between Alastair Campbell and the Number 10 press office on the one side, and the journalist Andrew Gilligan and the BBC on the other. They locked horns for months over the journalist's claim that the September 2002 dossier on Iraq issued by the British Government had been edited by Number 10, to give greater emphasis to the claim that the Iraqi regime possessed weapons of mass destruction that could be deployed within 45 minutes, if so ordered. That claim of exaggeration, and the vigorous denial by Number 10 that its inclusion in the dossier had been politically motivated and opposed by the intelligence community, produced a summer of headlines, select committee investigations and the tragic death of the BBC's main source for the story. The argument itself was largely a sideshow, in that it deflected public attention away from the causes of the invasion to the quality of the reporting upon it; but it did keep in the public eye the central issue of the credibility of government claims that the continuing absence of any weapons finds in post-war Iraq continually raised.[48]

In the absence of this 'smoking gun', the defenders of the war increasingly dropped back as month followed month into one or more of three recognizable postures: a defence of their previous justifications, a reordering of their importance and a respecification of some of their content.

The main response was dogged defence. President Bush provided one in September 2003, telling the American people that, by invading Iraq, the USA was 'rolling back the terrorist threat to civilization, not on the fringes of its influence, but at the heart of its power' since Iraq was now 'the central front' in the war on terrorism.[49] He provided a second defence before the UN Security Council that same month, telling the world leaders assembled there that 'the regime of Saddam Hussein cultivated ties to terror while it built weapons of mass destruction'. Before the UN, Bush paraded the invasion as the logical outcome of legitimate international concerns. With a sophistry rare in his public utterances, he defended his policies as though they were the UN's own:

> The Security Council was right to be alarmed. The Security Council was right to demand that Iraq destroy its illegal weapons and prove that it had done so. The Security Council was right to vow serious consequences if Iraq refused to comply. And because there were consequences, because a coalition of nations acted to defend the peace, and the credibility of the United Nations, Iraq is free, and today we are joined by representatives of a liberated people.[50]

Vice-President Cheney provided yet another line of defence before a conservative think-tank in Washington earlier in the summer, accusing those critical of the war of practising 20–20 hindsight. 'At a safe remove from the danger', he said, 'some are now trying to cast doubt upon the decision to liberate Iraq, but those who do so have an obligation to answer this question: how could any responsible leader have ignored the Iraqi threat?' He then rehearsed again the military underpinnings of that threat, insisting that prior to the invasion the regime in Baghdad had been in possession of chemical and biological weapons, illegal missiles and 'if left unchecked ... probably a nuclear weapon during this decade'.[51] 'Didn't you say yourself, in February 2001', Judy Woodruff asked Colin Powell in September, 'that we'd kept him contained, kept him in a box?' 'Yes', Powell replied:

> We tried to keep him bottled up, but bottled up doesn't mean gone away. It means bottled up and still a danger. And 9/11, it seemed to us, pulled the cork out of that bottle, and it was a danger and a risk we no longer wish to take.[52]

That was Tony Blair's public position too: that Saddam Hussein was too dangerous to leave corked up in that way. So in relation to the claims made in the September 2002 dossier, as he told the Liaison Committee in July, 'I do stand by the essential case ... I have absolutely no doubt at all that we will find evidence of weapons of mass destruction programmes, no doubt at all.'[53] He put down the failure to find them so far to the quality and skill of their concealment by Saddam Hussein prior to the war, an argument given a bizarre tweak by his Foreign Secretary in earlier evidence to a parallel committee. For Jack Straw pointed the finger of responsibility not only at the pre-war Saddam Hussein but also at the post-war one, arguing that coalition forces had yet to find weapons of mass destruction because local information on their hiding places was still not forthcoming: and it was not forthcoming because of the fear, among would-be informants, that Saddam Hussein would return to power. 'There are immense difficulties', he told the committee, 'particularly at this time, in creating a safe, secure and confident environment in which the right people feel confident in talking about programmes ... the sense of fear that Saddam could still be somewhere is very strong.'[54] Casuistry was much in vogue in governing circles in the middle of 2003.[55]

If that was not enough, the defenders of the war also shifted ground in several ways. There was a certain verbal slippage. The defence shifted from the existence of weapons of mass destruction to one of 'weapons of mass destruction *programs*', and then on to 'the capability' to develop such programs.[56] Ministerial spokespeople became adept at denying the significance of the change in terminology, but the change persisted nonetheless. Issues of morality, explicitly made secondary in the run-up to the invasion, now began to take centre stage. 'The UK should be proud of what it has done to rid Iraq of Saddam Hussein', the Prime Minister told the BBC. 'The dead and the missing', Straw said, 'are the most painful reminder of Saddam Hussein's brutal regime.'[57] And there was some challenging of the historical record: 'Some of our critics have tried to put into our mouths', the Foreign Secretary told the Foreign Affairs Committee, 'words and criteria we never ever used. We did not use the words "immediate" or "imminent" . . . We did not use that because plainly the evidence did not justify that. We did say that there was a "current and serious" threat and I stand by that completely.'[58]

But where the Foreign Secretary chose to stand, the Committee declined to follow. Such casuistry did not persuade them. They came back in this way:

> It is a matter of judgement whether a 'current and serious threat' is 'very different' in public perception from an 'imminent' or 'immediate' one, particularly when coupled with the Government's statement in its September 2002 dossier that 'intelligence indicates that the Iraqi military are able to deploy chemical or biological weapons within 45 minutes of an order to do so'. It is also notable that the danger of delaying military intervention in Iraq, including to Britain's own security, was a central theme of the Prime Minister's speech in the House of Commons of 18 March 2003 – on the eve of war.[59]

For in truth none of these word games, or the 'red herring' of the BBC/Campbell row, could answer the five powerful questions that Robin Cook put in his written memorandum to the Foreign Affairs Committee:

1   Why is there such a difference between the claims made before the war and the reality established after the war?
2   Did the Government itself come to doubt these claims before the war?
3   Could biological or chemical agents have fallen into the hands of terrorists since the war?
4   Why did we not allow the UN weapons inspectors back into Iraq?
5   Does the absence of weapons of mass destruction undermine the legal basis of the war?

There was more noise than light in London and Washington in the summer and autumn of 2003. No light on these five key questions: just the noise of chickens coming home to roost and of politicians grabbing at straws.

Motives and World Views

If one government has the desire, as Tony Blair made clear that his had, to stand 'shoulder to shoulder' to another, it is essential that their respective shoulders should be broadly congruent in shape and height. Yet throughout the entirety of this Iraq saga, US and UK shoulders were never entirely symmetrically aligned. There were always differences of perspective, of priority and of language at play whenever the two governments addressed their common concerns. Whenever George Bush and Tony Blair shared a platform, there could be no mistaking their different capacities with the English language. Everyone saw that – and many felt that Blair was simply putting an intellectual and moral gloss on what George Bush clearly lacked the linguistic and cerebral capacities to do for himself. But to formulate it in that way is to imply that both governments were on exactly the same line of exactly the same page whenever they spoke, and that the only differences in play between them at those moments were differences of presentational quality and style. There were such differences, it is true, but they were not the only ones. The differences in styles of delivery between Bush and Blair were also reflective of genuine differences in the substance of what each was trying to deliver.

Differences in Motives

This gap between the motives and concerns of the two governments was not just restricted to the issue of Israel and the Palestinians, or to the use of the UN in post-Hussein Iraq, though the gaps there were large and significant ones. The gap between them was a feature of the whole invasion story, and one that was very evident throughout to those of us uniquely positioned to watch its unfolding from both sides of the Atlantic. Read the UK press, listen to UK ministers, and the invasion was part of a global morality tale. But watch the US media, listen to Republican politicians in the United States, and the invasion was part of an entirely different story altogether: one largely denuded of high moral tone, one fuelled rather by a US determination to put second-ranking powers into line and to reassert the power of the USA as a global player. Tony Blair might present the invasion of Iraq – indeed he did – as 'a Third Way war', insisting in the *Guardian* that

> Our task should not be to shrink from full involvement in the battle against weapons of mass destruction and terrorism, but to broaden the agenda – to insist that there is as much effort shown in pursuing peace in the Middle East, in action on world poverty, Africa and climate change.[1]

But the Middle East apart, there was no such broadening of the agenda in Washington; and because there was not, it is vital to explore the differences in motives here, and to anchor those differences in distinctly British and American traditions of politics and policy.

For it may well be – it almost certainly is – the case that the motives taking the USA and UK into Iraq were different in each capital from the very outset of the process. It is actually quite hard to fathom the underlying US ones, for all the speed with which both defenders and critics of the Bush Administration now pontificate upon them. At the very least, however, they seem firmly anchored in a neo-conservative view of US foreign policy as hard-nosed and self-serving, and in a particularly Bush-family bit of unfinished business. As we saw in Part 1 of this study, what seems to have been immediately catalytic to the present conflict was the presence in the foreign-policy command posts of this Bush Administration of that group of policy-makers from the first Bush presidency, who had then been too junior to see the full implementation of a strategy of regime change in Baghdad. This is the group that includes Donald Rumsfeld, Paul Wolfowitz and Richard Perle.[2] It was they who developed their theory of pre-emptive defence – in fact the newly labelled 'Bush doctrine' was first laid out by them as early as 1992. It was they (along with Condoleezza Rice) who signed up to the famous 1998 open letter to President Clinton advocating militarily imposed regime change in Baghdad.[3] It was they who triggered the move from Afghanistan to Iraq that was embedded in Bush's 'axis of evil' speech.

Yet paradoxically, if that 'axis' actually existed, Iraq was the least developed of the three in terms of weapons of mass destruction. North Korea was clearly the most advanced and the most internationally volatile; and even Iran had more nuclear weapon potentiality than Iraq. The US intelligence community conceded all this on a regular basis; and yet US foreign policy was focused militarily on Iraq alone, so other motives must also have been at play throughout.

Completing unfinished business was undoubtedly one of them. Possibly the desire for a permanent US military presence in the Middle East was a second (that is still in dispute). Certain corporate needs and oil interests may be a third motive, and much has been made of them in critical accounts of the US rush to war. The importance and impact of oil interests is highly controversial here: both those of specific oil companies, and of oil as a general concern of the US and UK administrations. In our judgement, those strategic concerns played a subordinate but supporting role in the Bush Administration's decision to go to war, and we suspect (though we cannot prove) that the previous involvement of key Administration figures in the oil industry predisposed them to military intervention in the region. But we can see no parallel forces directly at work on the UK Government. Oil may be part of the American story here; but we don't see it as being in any significant way part of the UK story. Although the extensive links between New Labour and BP certainly give rise to misgivings about potential influence, the 'it's all about oil' argument seems to us too simplistic by far.[4] Certainly, the desire to send a loud and clear message about US power and the willingness to use it was a fourth and far more explicit motive: what one journalist rather inelegantly but no doubt accurately referred to as 'kicking some Arab fanny'.[5]

On the surface, and by contrast, the motives of the UK Government throughout this sorry saga have apparently been both clear and laudable. Tony Blair took a huge personal political risk himself in allying his Government so firmly with the Bush Administration, but it was one that was fully in line (as we will argue in more detail later in this chapter) with his Christian-inspired sense of the global importance of a Third Way international presence. For New Labour has been working hard, as he said in the *Guardian* article that was quoted earlier, on more than Iraq. It has been working hard on ways of 'cancelling third world debt, aid as a proportion of GDP and devising a strategy for development'.[6] Indeed, Tony Blair is on record as wanting to 'reorder this world' in a more humane way. He used his party conference speech immediately after 9/11 – one he reportedly wrote himself – to link his opposition to bin Laden and the Taliban to a wider call for human dignity and social justice on a global scale. In a speech tinged by emotions released by the horror of 9/11, and characterized by a large dose of unanchored moralizing, Blair told the delegates:

> I believe that this is a fight for freedom. And I want to make it a fight for justice too. Justice not only to punish the guilty. But justice to bring those same values of democracy and freedom to people round the world. And I mean: freedom, not only in the narrow sense of personal liberty but in the broader sense of each individual having the economic and social freedom to develop their potential to the full. That is what community means, founded on the equal worth of all. The starving, the wretched, the dispossessed, the ignorant, those living in want and squalor from the deserts of northern Africa to the slums of Gaza, to the mountain ranges of Afghanistan: they too are our cause. This is a moment to seize. The kaleidoscope has been shaken, the pieces are in flux. Soon they will settle again. Before they do let us reorder this world around us and use modern science to provide prosperity to all. Science can't make that choice for us. Only the moral power of a world acting as a community can.[7]

A similar sense of moral purpose accompanied all the Blair defences of the invasion itself, and clearly sustained the Prime Minister at moments when his political gamble appeared to be coming unstuck. Commentators sympathetic to his dilemma reported on his willingness to defend his decisions on Iraq before his Maker, and commended him for it.[8] What they commented on less was the liberal imperialism and residual Atlanticism with which his Maker would be confronted during that defence. For here was a New Labour leader fully in tune with Labour leaders in the past, prepared again to send UK troops off on a global mission with the United States, the alliance wrapped once more in the sanctimonious language of civilizing purposes. Nowhere in that frame of thought did there appear to be the slightest space for the recognition that the arrival of UK and US troops in the streets of Iraq would be as unpalatable to most Iraqis as would the arrival of Arab troops in the streets of Washington and London, no matter how well-intentioned their presence there. Imperialism is imperialism, after all, and is invariably experienced as such. Global governance is something else, and something better: but the USA and the UK did not turn up in Iraq this time with even the fig leaf of a UN mandate to cover their private purposes.

In any event, and as we have said, it is not clear that the private purposes behind the US presence on the streets of Baghdad were and are as unsullied as those of the Messianic British in Basra. In truth, the other motive for the UK Government's decision to stay close to the Americans – at the cost of its European alliances – does appear to have been to keep the USA as close as possible to the multilateralism of the earlier Bush Administration in the first Gulf War, and to slow the pace and range of the current Bush Administration's unilateral militarism. The clearest documentation of that set of concerns appears in Peter Stothard's *30 Days*, where he reports the existence of a list of points on the London–Washington–Baghdad interplay, drawn up in September 2002 by the Prime Minister, 'to which he and his aides would regularly return'. The list is worth reproducing in full:

- Saddam Hussein's past aggression, present support for terrorism and future ambitions made him a clear threat to his enemies. He was not the only goal, but he was a threat nonetheless.
- The United States and Britain were among his enemies.
- The people of the United States, still angered by the 11 September attacks, still sensing unfinished business from the first Gulf War twelve years before, would support a war on Iraq.
- Gulf War 2 – President George W. Bush vs. Saddam Hussein – would happen whatever anyone else said or did.
- The people of Britain, continental Europe and most of the rest of the world would not even begin to support a war unless they had a say through the United Nations.
- It would be more damaging to long-term world peace and security if the Americans alone defeated Saddam Hussein than if they had international support to do so.[9]

The list is a truly remarkable one. If true, it tells us that even in September 2002 Tony Blair was resigned to the inevitability of war. Clare Short may not have been right to claim that the decision to go to war was agreed between Bush and Blair in September, but she seems to have been right in sensing Blair's willingness to go along with an American military move even that early in the struggle for a UN resolution. The list also demonstrates the Blair determination to stay with the Americans, and to hold them to a multilateral politics. But if that was the Blair intention, it singularly failed – and then the list indicates the choice that the Prime Minister had eventually to face. Which point in the list was to be the breaker for Blair: the penultimate one or the final one? Events proved that it was the final one that prevailed. As Martin Kettle put it, the list shows that in the end Britain 'went to war to keep on the right side of Washington'.[10]

Differences in World Views

So if Tony Blair's involvement in, and enthusiastic endorsement of, the Iraqi invasion cannot be explained by any natural and close fit between the wider aims of his foreign policy and those of the Bush Administration, how is it to be explained? Our view is that the key to his foreign policy, like the key to the foreign policy of Labour leaders in the past, lies in the overall world view that he and they bring to the totality of their policy agenda – and as such has to be understood *sui generis*. Tony Blair's role in the Iraqi story has to be understood, that is, not by looking outwards to the pulling force of Washington; it has to be understood by looking inwards, to the framing premises of past and present Labour politics. His role, and that of his ministers, has to be grasped as the natural outgrowth of their general understanding of the world, a general understanding that gives a unity to the thrust of their domestic *and* their foreign policy. It has also to be grasped as the outgrowth of legacies left in the mindsets of contemporary Labour leaders by the world views prevalent in the minds of previous generations of those same leaders. New Labour is not as new as it likes to claim. Its general analysis of the world, and of the role of states within that world, has new emphases and inflections, but it also carries within it large elements of imperialism and Atlanticism left behind by the thinking and practice of Labour leaders in the past. *It is the fusion of those new inflections and old legacies that holds the key to why, as we write, UK troops police the streets of Basra.*[11]

So to get to grips with the underlying causes of what happened here, we need to go beyond a superficial and personalized explanation of why the UK Government broke with its European allies and threw in its lot with a US administration whose leaders held a quite different set of values and general understandings of the world. We need to probe the history and character of the Labour Party itself. Students of British Labour (ourselves included) have too often in the past separated domestic and foreign policy as objects of analysis. To understand Blair's Messianic move to Basra, we have to bring those separate studies together. The question, of course, is 'how?' and we suggest that there is much mileage to be had from standing back from the detail of the Iraqi story for a moment, to build some general models of Labour politics through which to isolate the manner in which foreign and domestic policy necessarily originate together. In our view, four such models are vital here, organized in a two-by-two matrix. To understand how New Labour took the UK to the invasion of Iraq, we need to see how an *Old Labour* model was challenged historically by a *Left-Labour* alternative, and how the legacies of that political confrontation now leave us with a new choice: between a *New Labour* understanding of the world that generates a foreign policy scarred by residues of imperialism and Atlanticism and yet still insists on resolute multilateralism, and Blair's new post-9/11 mentality – what we will call *defiant internationalism*. We will use the first three models in this chapter to help shed light on the fourth – Blair's startling embrace of a unilateral military intervention that imperils British power and prestige and that defies his own core principles of interdependence and cooperation. Read in tandem with our previous account of Blair's justifications for going to war, the first three models will help both to characterize and to explain the thinking behind the decision to invade Iraq. The analysis of these models will show how the selective appropriation of diverse Labour Party legacies critically shaped Blair's moral sensibilities and world view, and will reveal points of fissure with Labour's heritage made by Blair once he had set his sights on war.

Labourism

Classic British Labourism (what New Labour more polemically calls 'Old Labour') may be located within the political framework broadly identified with European social democracy, as that developed in Western Europe after the Second World War. For some three decades, a tacit alliance between the organized working class and large-scale business created a set of distributive cross-class growth coalitions and political bargains which were institutionalized in nationally specific 'post-war settlements', which then set the framework for a general understanding of European party competition, political economy and broad policy orientations. In the heyday of this model (roughly 1945 to the first oil crisis of 1973), states intervened extensively to regulate economies, promote economic growth and secure nearly full employment while expanding welfare provision. Within the model, Keynesian economics provided the rationale for a vigorous, activist governmental stance to ensure aggregate demand through high levels of spending, which would in turn stimulate economic growth; and in consequence the harmonious, positive-sum politics of class compromise became crystallized in the tacit agreements of the post-war settlement, and a period of sustained growth replaced traditional zero-sum class-based conflict.

On one end of the spectrum of variants of this classical model stood its most robust case: Swedish social democracy. There, the electoral strength of the Social Democratic Party (SAP), combined with labour corporatism and solidaristic wage-bargaining strategies, led to a vast array of comprehensive, egalitarian, redistributive and universal welfare provisions. On the other pole of the model, by contrast, stood the 'Labourism' that serves as the dramatic foil for Blair's New Labour agenda. British Labourism was both weaker than other European social democratic models in its institutional reach (the National Economic Development Council was no Commissariat Général du Plan) and less robust in its policy aims (no serious consideration was given to worker participation as in German co-determination or works councils, and there was never even a hint of collective share-ownership through the build-up of wage-earner funds, as in Sweden's Meidner Plan). Moreover, although British tripartism, particularly in the area of incomes policies, involved the characteristic corporatist practice of state-bargaining with peak associations, its episodic and one-sided nature (involving labour more than business) and the low durability of the bargains struck locate Britain very much on the edge of the corporatist model originally designed for Sweden, Austria, Switzerland, Belgium and the Netherlands.[12] But nonetheless, though it represented a minimalist form of the model, Britain's Labourism is still best understood as part of this general kind of post-war social democratic politics: one predicated on the building and sustaining of class compacts within autonomous and competing nation-states.

That model may have been international in scope, but it was generally domestic in focus. It certainly was in the British case. For it has been rightly observed that despite the recurrent strength of liberal internationalists among the party faithful, 'the political structure accepted by labourism in which to conduct its social and economic struggle [was] the structure of the nation state'.[13] This is a telling point, since it identifies Labourism not only as reformist but, equally important, as statist. Moreover, it is undoubtedly the case that although the precise interplay of 'nation' and 'class' in the policy stance of the Labour Party has varied historically, the party's pursuit of class interests has always been mediated through the lens of national interests, and more often than not subordinated to them.[14] We can thus add nationalist to statist and the die is cast. The Labour party in its Old Labour form was inexorably positioned by its approach to domestic affairs to privilege British interests above class interests, and to see the defence of state and nation as its paramount responsibility – the test of Labour's bona fides as a legitimate party of government.

During the Second World War, the party's statist and nationalist impulses, combined with its adoption of dominant liberal economic doctrine, were decisively reinforced in the broader political-cultural realm. As one observer noted about the proclivity of the Attlee Government to subordinate domestic reforms to great power imperatives: 'To a greater extent than is generally understood, Labour's mentality had been stamped from its inception by values and beliefs derived from the established national culture.'[15] The recipe for post-war Labourism was complete. Taken together, the statist predilection combined with the adoption of dominant national cultural values fostered traditionalism in the foreign policy orientations as the dominant position within the party throughout the post-Second World War era. There were, to be sure, deep currents of internationalism and anti-militarism within the ranks of the Labour Party. Nevertheless, when push came to shove, when Britain faced security threats and the external demands of Great Power politics, internationalism evaporated and the vast majority of the Labour Party supported national war efforts. This overwhelming tendency for the party to rally around flag and country – inspired by powerful political and cultural instincts and reinforced by the mandates of party politics – was demonstrated by the party's willingness to join governing coalitions in both world wars. The support for national war efforts was reaffirmed in party manifestos issued in the aftermath of the First World War, the Second World War and the Korean War, in which the party rightly asserted its contributions to wartime success.[16] Despite subtle shifts with time and circumstances, Labour's traditional foreign policy can be reduced to a set of core permanent objectives transcending party preferences: 'self-regarding promotion of national interests, defense of a far-flung imperial and commercial network, and management of a European balance as a condition of British security – all backed, whenever necessary, by the application of force.'[17]

In the crystallization of this mindset – as in the demonstration that foreign policy serves as a powerful rudder in setting the course and determining the party's fortunes – the experience of the 1945–51 Labour Government was especially notable. What is most interesting is that, on the domestic front, the Attlee Government was committed to what passes for socialism in the British context: to the extensive nationalization of industry, the formation and institutional consolidation of the welfare state, the promise of full employment, a dose of democratic state planning and the redistribution of income and wealth to the poor and the working class. This programmatic agenda lent the 1945–51 Government its radical edge – all the more so in the retrospective gaze shaped by the subsequent Wilson–Callaghan Governments – and it was defended as 'socialist' by the Labour Left at least through to the 1960s.[18] Yet, at the same time, the Attlee Government was seduced by the traditional siren song of national grandeur, which obliged it, even during the hard economic times that existed, to imperil its domestic agenda to secure its imperial designs. As the India Secretary Lord Listowel observed about the former union leader turned Foreign Secretary Ernest Bevin, he was 'at heart an old fashioned imperialist, keener to expand than contract the Empire'.[19] The Government's ultimate commitment to the interests of the state, defined as the projection of British influence in the world, was confirmed by its resolute determination to maintain a military force in excess of one million men in the Middle East and to provide the UK with its own nuclear capability, whatever the drain on the exchequer, and however unlikely its operational utility. As Bevin insisted against Attlee's reservations about the need for a British atomic bomb, 'We've got to have a bloody Union Jack flying on top of it.' Bevin was the real force for the bomb and its most effective advocate, viewing at least nominally independent nuclear capability as the precondition for Great Power status. 'For the "working-class John Bull" it was a matter of simple patriotism to put a Union Jack on the atomic bomb', the historian Peter Hennessy wrote; 'Great powers had to have great weapons.'[20] And thus it was that traditionalism in foreign policy so distorted a socialist conception of class interest that the patriotic and pugnacious figure of John Bull, the eighteenth-century cartoon character who remained a hyper-patriotic symbol of British nationalism, came to stand for working-class interests.

The traditionalist orientation of Old Labour's foreign policy and its basic ingredients changed little in the intervening years, although changes in the international context, of course, required adjustments. Through the 1950s, the left in the Labour Party was soundly defeated on the foreign policy and defence grounds it sought to emphasize: the rearmament of Germany and unilateral nuclear disarmament. As Stephen Haseler observed, 'the fifties was an empty time for socialism within the Labour Party'.[21] It was a sign of the times, and of the drift of Labourism decisively towards state and nation, that the foreign policy traditionalists and domestic policy revisionists who dominated the party in opposition struggled to establish the claim that a left-wing party with a working-class base could match the Cold War zeal and nationalism of the right. In the 1960s, the commitment to Great Power status shifted from a desire for imperial expansion to the playing of a critical strategic role as an offshore balancer in Europe[22] framed by a 'special relationship' with the United States to offset German and French dominance of the European Community. Despite such subtle modifications, however, throughout the post-war period Labour's foreign policy traditionalism meant the putting of nation above class, a sustained commitment to the projection of British power abroad and an especially strong commitment to NATO and the Atlantic alliance. The commitment to a traditional foreign policy presupposed as an article of faith the determination to preserve robust options for the use of force – even the expensive maintenance of the full triad of conventional, tactical nuclear and strategic nuclear weapons, despite popular opposition and enormous economic pressures throughout the Wilson–Callaghan Governments of the 1970s.[23]

It should be emphasized as well that Labour foreign policy traditionalists put great store in massaging the relationship between prime ministers and party leaders and American presidents. Despite sharp differences over the Vietnam War and Wilson's refusal to send even a symbolic British force to Vietnam – which put considerable strains on the Atlantic alliance – he worked hard to preserve a close relationship with the USA, and in large part for this reason pumped very significant resources into NATO. James Callaghan was determined to reverse what he perceived as Edward Heath's commitment to Europe, which he held responsible for weakening Britain's ties with the USA. Working to undo the damage to relations with the United States that resulted from Labour's support for unilateral nuclear disarmament through much of the 1980s (until its defeat in the 1987 general election prompted a major policy review), Labour Party leader Neil Kinnock supported the Gulf War in 1991, a development which strengthened the relationship between the Labour Party and the US Administration. And in a haunting prelude to Tony Blair's wartime alliance with George W. Bush, after a meeting in Washington with President George H. W. Bush in July 1991, the Labour Party leader, upon his return to London, proclaimed: 'There are no differences at all between us in the areas we discussed.'[24] On the assumption that Iraq was high on the agenda, Kinnock's testimony is a fitting valedictory to Labour's traditional foreign policy and an alarming presentiment of things to come.

Old Labour's foreign policy stance can be summarized thus:

Framework 1   *British Labourism: traditional foreign policy*

Promote the British state and its national interests, above class and party, by an active defence of imperial and commercial interests and the effective management of a balance of power in Europe. Britain's role as an offshore balancer of Europe and as a Great Power to be enhanced by a dedicated commitment to an Atlantic alliance and a robust participation in NATO. Britain's international status and security require the commitment to a global military capability and the willingness to use force, backed by the full triad of conventional, tactical nuclear and strategic nuclear weapons.

The Left-Labour Critique

Although dominated in the post-Second World War period by such a set of traditionally statist and nationalist foreign policy (and domestic revisionist) orientations, the British Left then, as now, was a rich hybrid. Certainly, it was far more diverse and vibrant than the standard characterization of British Labourism, as shallow European social democracy reveals. Although dominated by the standard welfare state traditions and statist Labourism associated with the post-war settlement, elements in the post-war British Left also drew inspiration from a range of alternative sources: the inspiration of syndicalist anti-capitalist working-class agitation mythologized by Chartism; the deeply religious appeals to 'brotherhood' and altruism of the International Labour Party (ILP) tradition; the Fabian goal of collectivism in every sphere of social and economic life; and the Christian socialist aim of cooperative society based on communal (or community) ownership, devoid of the antagonisms fostered by competitive capitalism.[25]

In the discussion of the New Labour model below, we will see that Tony Blair draws very strongly on the Christian socialist tradition and on the normative appeals to community in particular. But before analysing the dominant New Labour paradigm, it is necessary to recapture the subversive socialist current in old-style Labourism that drew on the more egalitarian, anti-capitalist, solidaristic and insurrectionary traditions within British socialism, particularly those most closely associated with the ILP tradition which in no small measure gave rise to the socialist foreign policy critique of both the inter-war and the immediate post-war period. Playing a decisive role in the formation and development of the Labour Party, the ILP was the dominant socialist group within the party until the rightist policy drift of the two Labour Governments in the inter-war period led to its decision to disaffiliate in 1932.[26] Most important here, as one scholar of Labour Party foreign policy emphasized, was the fact that the ILP had a 'decisive impact on Labour after 1918'. The ILP's 'systematic anti-capitalism – especially in connection with the origins of the war and the precariousness of the peace – was incorporated wholesale into Labour's inter-war foreign policy pronouncements.'[27] Thus, the socialist foreign policy critique of traditional Labour foreign policy took a deep hold in the inter-war years, as did the broader claim that foreign and domestic policy were integrally connected and animated by an anti-capitalist critique. As even Arthur Henderson, Foreign Secretary in the 1929 Labour Government, put it: 'Labour's policy at home and abroad forms one organic whole, because our foreign policy is a function of our domestic policy and both spring from our faith that the future belongs to Socialism.'[28]

Four core principles of that inter-war socialist foreign policy have been aptly identified:

- *Internationalism* (as the antidote to a foreign policy intended to advance parochial national interest, contributing to an inherently unstable and conflict-ridden international order). In institutional terms, internationalism includes a commitment to multilateral institutions, starting with support for a strengthened and democratized League of Nations, to preserve international peace and act as a counterweight to myopic national interests.[29]
- *International working-class solidarity* (the view that organized cross-border working-class cooperation was a critical resource for preventing war, including pro-Soviet sentiment and rejection of the dominant anti-Communist streak in the party).
- *Anti-capitalism* (the core rejection of British foreign policy as an instrument for securing profitable markets for investment).
- *Anti-militarism* (an antipathy to power politics and the use of force and the conviction that real security must rest on morality, open diplomacy, international cooperation and, ultimately, the victory of international socialism).[30]

However profoundly the international context has been transformed in the intervening years, we nonetheless see much to recommend in these principles. And like them or not, these principles have sustained powerful critical movements within the Labour Party across the generations. The *Keep Left* mobilization after 1945, calling for a 'third way' or 'third force' between Soviet communism and American capitalism and arguing that Britain should take a moral lead in foreign affairs, was, in many ways, 'a tamer echo of the ILP Left which had harried Ramsay MacDonald'.[31] Rejecting the Anglo-American alliance at the heart of traditional foreign policy, the third force approach called for British leadership in a social democratic, neutralist camp that would be powerful enough to guarantee UK security and prevent the otherwise inevitable war that would be triggered by Cold War tensions.[32] The Campaign for Nuclear Disarmament (CND), formed in 1958, reinvigorated the third force, unilateralist and anti-militarist orientation of the powerful left foreign policy critique and, making its provenance unmistakably clear, it featured Michael Foot, one of the authors of *Keep Left*, as a founding member.[33] And a less anti-capitalist but strongly pacifist and anti-nuclear orientation re-emerged forcefully in the 1980s. Between 1981 and 1986, by sizeable majorities, Labour Party conferences repeatedly passed motions that opposed the siting of cruise missiles with nuclear warheads on British soil, supported the removal of American nuclear bases from Britain and committed the party (briefly as it transpired) to unilateral nuclear disarmament.

This Left-Labour critique of the traditional foreign policy of Old Labour can be summarized thus:

Framework 2   British Labourism: the socialist foreign policy critique

Promote the advance of socialism and the advance of the Left within the Labour Party by insisting that foreign and domestic policy are integrally and organically connected by a set of core principles: internationalism, international working-class solidarity, anti-capitalism and anti-militarism. Britain's foreign policy and security interests to be best advanced by the projection abroad of clear ethical principles for the conduct of foreign policy, a commitment to third force neutralism and the building of multilateral institutions, a rejection of nuclear options and support for unilateral nuclear disarmament.

New Labour

What can be said about New Labour's relationship to these various shades of old-style Labourism, in both its domestic and foreign policy dimensions? For a start, New Labour strategists and stalwarts refuse to be trapped in the downward spiral of electoral fortunes that they believe would inevitably follow from narrow appeals to a politically and numerically diminished working class. Hence, they have quite intentionally and systematically broken the linkage between party and class, making clear that New Labour's modernizing appeal, above all, denies that the party is the representative of the working class. Labourist social democracy ('Old Labour') appears as the dramatic foil for Blair's modernizing agenda and, in terms of institutional arrangements, New Labour's signature innovations are intended, as its architects make clear, to reverse the tendency of Labour to 'provide centralised, statist solutions to every social and economic problem'.[34] At the same time, New Labour strategy reduces the salience of distributive politics with its forthright insistence on fiscal prudence; and, in fact, by appealing to individuals across the spectrum of class positions, New Labour has attempted entirely to sever the historic connection between class-based material interests and politics. You can hardly get any less old-style socialist than that.

However, New Labour's relationship to traditional European social democracy and British Labourism is more complex and nuanced than it might at first appear. For both historic legacies and voter expectations have made it difficult for the party modernizers to achieve a radical break with the policy approaches and institutional orientations of the institutional-collectivist Old Labour model. In consequence, New Labour policy exhibits some critical areas of continuity with traditional Labourism – not least in its continuing dedication to the caring issues, in its expansive commitments to healthcare and education and in the persistence of a taken-for-granted egalitarianism in its normative orientations. Moreover, and while rejecting the institutional dimensions of European social democracy and the more militant, syndicalist and anti-capitalist traditions within Labourism, New Labour still draws very strongly on its normative claims in general, and on the Christian socialist tradition in particular. In fact, among the historic strands of British Labourism, the Christian socialist aim of a cooperative and more communal (community-based) society devoid of the antagonisms fostered by competitive capitalism has become an especially significant component of Blair's socialist vision. It also acted as an important source for the ethical dimension of New Labour's foreign policy, before 9/11 and Iraq changed all that.

But not everything is continuity here, of course. Clearly, for Blair, even though a set of normative predispositions associated with the Christian socialist strand of British social democracy frames the underlying ethical domain of both domestic and foreign policy, a particular reading of globalization justifies New Labour's rupture with classic European social democracy and with Labourism. From Blair's perspective, globalization means, first and foremost, the emergence of a global economic system beyond the control of any given state, in which competitiveness, comparative advantage and growth are seen to require strict adherence to the credos of fiscal and monetary stability and neo-liberalism. With such a view of the world, the role of government shifts away from traditional Keynesian demand policies favoured by Old Labour and towards a set of policies intended to create, above all else, a favourable environment for domestic as well as foreign investment. In policy terms, this approach endorses flexibility in the production system to improve competitiveness and attract foreign investment, creates partnerships with business to encourage long-term investment, and supports training, high-technology skill acquisition and welfare reform to foster job-creation. In short, for New Labour the neo-liberal anti-regulatory bias of the monetary and production regime circumscribes government policy. Indeed and overall, it is probably fair to say that the imperatives of globalization have *pulled* New Labour economic policy in the same direction that their interpretation of globalization – and broader ideological, normative, intellectual and strategic-electoral thinking – *pushes* them. New Labour leaders want to create in the UK an economy in which both local and overseas investors wish to place their capital,[35] and they believe that they can do that best by establishing a close and enabling partnership with UK-based industry, by putting its 'relations with the trade unions on a modern footing where they accept they can get fairness but not favours from a Labour government'[36] and by prioritizing the achievement of international competitiveness on the basis of 'higher quality, skill, innovation and reliability'.[37]

The New Labour leadership of Tony Blair and his extremely influential Chancellor of the Exchequer, Gordon Brown, accept globalization as a fact of life – not as a set of transformations to be lamented, but as a set of challenges to be met and mastered through pragmatic and innovative policies. New Labour's reading of globalization justifies its decisive break with Labourism as outdated and unworkable for any number of reasons. The explicit social democratic commitments to Keynesianism and social protection presupposed the capacity of nation-states to draft their own models for governing the economy and autonomously control their economic destinies through the mobilization of support from domestic coalitions. With this implicit, unquestioned and now unworkable assumption of national autonomy jettisoned, New Labour places globalization front and centre, and embraces the world of complex and overlapping sovereignty and intensified interdependence. The first critical postulate of New Labour's geopolitical strategy is revealed by this stance on globalization: its pragmatic acquiescence to a world in which the British state cannot control outcomes, expressed as a commitment to *interdependence*. This vision correlated precisely with the internationalism and multilateralism that framed the initial New Labour reconfiguration of UK foreign policy on ethical lines, but it should not be forgotten that Blair's dictum of global interdependence also anchored his hard-edged advocacy for the military campaign in Kosovo.

New Labour's approach to foreign policy – what earlier we called *warlike humanitarianism* or, following the work of John Mearsheimer we might now call *offensive multilateralism*[38] – is powerfully located both in New Labour's interpretation of the dictates of national interest in the global era and in its reading of the bundle of traditions that historically constitute Labourism. Viewed through a comparative lens in the context of European social democracy, British Labourism looks a-theoretical and pragmatic. It appears non-interventionist in

its approach to Keynesian demand management and in its unwilling-
ness to challenge the abiding neo-liberal character of British economic
management strategies.[39] All these policy orientations set British social
democracy apart from its continental European counterparts. The
British case, however, represents an important alternative precisely
because its institutional underdevelopment has always been counter-
balanced by a well-articulated and robust ethical vision, a matter of
great importance for the analysis here. In an important sense, the
comparative advantage of British social democracy lies in the ethical
dimension that paradoxically gives it both depth and ambiguity. New
Labour is making good use of this opening as it works to reinvent an
ethos for the Labour Party.

We can see this reworking in a carefully crafted speech by Tony
Blair to the Fabian Society. There, Blair argued that the 'ethical basis
of socialism' – as distinct from what he called its 'economic dogma' –
is the only socialist foundation that has stood the test of time and
survived the collapse of communism. Blair then described his conception of the normative basis of New Labour's concept of socialism:

> This socialism is based on a moral assertion that individuals are inter-
> dependent, that they owe duties to one another as well as themselves,
> that the good society backs up the efforts of the individuals within it,
> and that common humanity demands that everyone be given a plat-
> form on which to stand. It has objective basis too, rooted in the belief
> that only by recognizing their interdependence will individuals flourish,
> because the good of each does depend on the good of all. This concept
> of socialism requires a form of politics in which we share responsibil-
> ity both to fight poverty, prejudice and unemployment, and to create
> the conditions in which we can truly build one nation.[40]

Blair's remarks capture New Labour's core normative themes: *interdependence* (rather than conflict); commonality of values and aims
defined in terms of *community* or humanity (but never in class terms);
and the *responsibility* of individual citizens (rather than – or linked
to – their rights or entitlements). There is considerable variation in
the explicit language and in the choice of normative traditions invoked
to supply the ethical moment in New Labour's model of government,
but the Christian socialist traditions provide insight into his moral
compass. Blair attributes his rejection both of a narrow Tory view of
self-interest and the determinism he associates with Marxism to his
Christian values. Very likely too, it was this Christian socialism that
inspired Blair's combination of toughness and moral righteousness as
a war leader which was revealed when he stood out as the strongest
advocate among NATO leaders for the air campaign in Kosovo: an

air campaign in pursuit of what he insisted was a war for humanitarian purposes – and an air campaign that he insisted had aggressively to pursue its objectives.[41]

Most importantly for our purposes, the Kosovo conflict created the context for Blair's explicit linkage of globalization with foreign and security policy in one of his most categorical statements of the guiding principles for British foreign (and domestic) policy. In a speech delivered in Chicago on the eve of NATO's fiftieth anniversary, Blair began a section on 'global interdependence' by emphasizing the broad geopolitical implications of globalization:

> Twenty years ago we would not have been fighting in Kosovo. We would have turned our backs on it. The fact that we are engaged is the result of a wide range of changes – the end of the Cold War, changing technology, the spread of democracy. But it is bigger than that. I believe the world has changed in a more fundamental way. Globalisation has transformed economies and our working practices. But globalisation is not just economic, it is a political and security phenomenon.[42]

Blair argued that isolationism was no longer an option: financial insecurity in Asia had destroyed jobs from Chicago to his own constituency in County Durham, and conflict in the Balkans had led to an influx of refugees in Germany as well as the United States. He extolled the 'impulse towards interdependence' and the 'new doctrine of international community', which he characterized as 'the explicit recognition that today more than ever before, we are mutually dependent, that national interest is to a significant extent governed by international collaboration and that we need a clear and coherent debate as to the direction this doctrine takes us in each field of international endeavour'.[43] Above all, Blair made very clear that New Labour's governing model – as well as its guiding ethical principles – cut both ways, in domestic as well as foreign affairs. In fact, it seems clear that in narratives of community it finds its moral voice and locates a comfortable 'third way' ethos to guide institutional and policy innovation. 'Community' is the normative glue that holds together the domestic and foreign policy components of New Labour, capturing the salutary blend of individuality (recast in the international realm as national interest), balanced by the interdependence that Blair considers to be the core of socialism. So, in Chicago, Blair was able to insist that:

> Just as within domestic politics, the notion of community – the belief that partnership and cooperation are essential to advance self-interest – is coming into its own . . . so it needs to find its international echo. Global

financial markets, the global environment, global security and disarmament issues: none of these can be solved without intense cooperation.[44]

Blair also noted the 'danger of letting wherever CNN roves be the
cattle prod to take a global conflict seriously', and argued instead
for the sustained effort to advance 'the principles of the doctrine of
international community and . . . the institutions that deliver them'.[45]
Without specifying the relevant principles much further, Blair called
for NATO to give serious focus to the lessons of Kosovo, for a review of the decision making process in the United Nations (and in
the Security Council in particular), and for the serious consideration
of third world debt.[46] For Blair, globalization – as a set of imperatives that mandate the historic Labour Party rupture with social
democracy – is indistinguishable from its ethical mission to build
community at home and to build international collaboration abroad.
Before 9/11 shifted Blair's perspective, and his commitment to Bush's
war in Iraq subverted New Labour's heady post-1997 foreign policy
vision, its guiding principles were clear.

Framework 3   New Labour: offensive multilateralism

Harness the forces of globalization and the practical realities of interdependence
to advance internationalism, multilateralism and cooperation in the economic,
environmental and security dimensions of foreign affairs. When necessary, advance humanitarian policy through resolute military means consonant with the
doctrine of international community and advance the strategic goal of enhancing
Britain's global power and prestige. Engage the questions of debt reduction and
institutional reform that are required to secure the aims of human rights, democratic governance and security.

New Labour: Defiant Internationalism

Chapter 4 has chronicled the transformation of Tony Blair's foreign
policy mindset, from the moment he adopted the terror attacks of
11 September 2001 as his (and the UK's) own problem. Here, it is
sufficient to note the enormity of the shift, once a combination
of laudable instincts and the fateful attraction of the Old Labour
model of imperialism and Atlanticism achieved an irresistible hold
over British foreign policy. Before 9/11, New Labour stood for a
coherent and progressive foreign policy framework, one that we
have just labelled 'offensive multilateralism'. By comparison, Blair's
post-9/11 foreign policy posture has been clumsy and ungainly. It has
retained an internationalist perspective, in that it has insisted that
Britain actively participate in a robust global agenda; but it has sacri-

ficed the multilateralism of New Labour's original vision to the Bush Administration's insistence that the USA alone call the tune, whether or not it pays the fiddler.

Of course we realize that however pivotal at the time, Blair's instinctive gesture to make the tragedy of 11 September 2001 a British tragedy, to express a unique empathy with America's anguish and to accept a responsibility to fight terrorism 'shoulder to shoulder' with the United States struck a resonant chord with the overwhelming majority of Britons (and Americans). In the shock and grief triggered by that event, it was clear that sacrifices would be expected – but it was not then immediately clear that among those sacrifices would be the surrender of the principles and aims that had hitherto guided New Labour's foreign policy. George Bush's State of the Union Address in January 2002 made it clear beyond all possible doubt that the war against terrorism would soon place Iraq firmly in the crosshairs of the US military, and drew from the UK Foreign Secretary the observation that, although the UK was no longer a superpower, it would continue to assert a 'pivotal role' in global affairs, including affairs in Iraq. Yet within months of that observation being made, it was also clear that foreign policy itself rotated on a single fixed axis, with the coordinates set in Arlington, Virginia, and not in London, and that no space for such a UK pivotal role would be tolerated by the policy-making establishment in Washington. George Bush's people, we might remember, were not immediately sure what to do with Tony Blair when first he came at them after 9/11. But one thing they were sure about, even then, was that it would be they, and not he, who would design their response to the terrorist attack upon them.

We will argue in the final chapter of this volume that throughout this sorry saga the UK Government should have insisted on conditional support for US policy, and should have applied strict 'red lines' that would have limited the blowback that is now coming from the implementation of unprincipled and wrongheaded American policy mandates: but it did not. Instead, by throwing in its lot with the Americans, and doing so in such an unconditional manner, the UK Government lost its pivotal geopolitical role. It missed its opportunity to shape a principled post-9/11 response to the new world of strategic cross-border terrorism, and it sacrificed the bold, innovative and forward-looking approach to foreign policy that was captured in New Labour's post-1997 commitments to multilateralism in foreign affairs. However deep the recoil in the UK against the terror attacks of 11 September, however powerful the empathy or steadfast the commitment to defeat terrorist groups, it must be remembered that British foreign policy retained the capacity to steer its own course; and yet in practice no such steering occurred. Critical shifts in policy could have been – and should have been – averted: but they were not. Time and again after 9/11, British foreign policy turned on the American pivot. Washington demanded support for a 'war' on terrorism. The UK concurred. Washington demanded that the war move from Afghanistan to Iraq. The UK concurred. Washington demanded that the Security Council become ensnared – and undermined – through dishonest manipulation of facts and by the pretext of insincere diplomatic overtures. The UK concurred. Washington decided that the war could commence without a second resolution. The UK concurred. Whatever reservations Blair had about each of these critical policy junctures, he still acquiesced, and he need not have done so.

What in consequence has become of Tony Blair's commitments to global community and the reform of global governance? As far as we can tell, they have been sacrificed to a new mindset that we might call *defiant internationalism*. It is a mindset characterized by a 'go for broke' risk-taking strategy to advance British interests and maximize national power, and paradoxically to do so in a world where nation-states are seen as having far less power than before. And it is a mindset that has enabled Tony Blair enthusiastically to join America's unilaterally designed and implemented war in Iraq, while simultaneously justifying that war by appeals to the international community, to the demands of interdependence and to a commitment to multilateral institutions, all of which have been damaged, perhaps irretrievably, by the actions thus justified. For now, whatever the cost, Blair is content to play Robin to Bush's Batman, fighting masked villains as loyal underling in the dynamic duo, and defying the international community, the nation and the party as he does so. His defiance is the product, we believe, of this fourth mindset.

Framework 4   New Labour: defiant internationalism

Rewrite foreign policy to meet the security threats of the post-9/11 order. The democratic preferences of nation and party – and the commitment to strengthen and reform the United Nations and especially the Security Council – must give way to the 'war on terrorism'. Whatever differences that may develop between the UK and USA (regarding the role of the Security Council, the linkage of the Israeli-Palestine conflict to the war in Iraq, the best mix of instruments to be used in fighting terrorism, the role of the United Nations in post-war 'nation-building', and so on) must all be subordinated to the Anglo-American alliance. War in Iraq is justified by the weapons of mass destruction threats of the Saddam Hussein regime as well as its record of horrific human rights abuses and defiance of the United Nations. British national interests and values are best advanced by its unique partnership with the United States.

PART III

THE ALTERNATIVE TO WAR

Reflections and Lessons

One of the very important points in this argument that needs re-emphasizing here is that we do recognize the force of the argument that after 9/11 the United States (and by association the UK) did acquire a new security problem. We do see that this new security problem did and does demand an entirely new form of defence. That argument seems entirely valid to us, and we will develop it in our concluding chapter as a key component in our proposal for an alternative foreign policy. The argument we have had with the US and UK Governments, as they responded to the events of 9/11, has not been that there should not have been a response. It has been, rather, that the response that was made was the incorrect one. We have argued, and will argue further here, that for the military of either country to invade Iraq in response to this new security agenda was and is entirely counter-productive. We have also argued that even if it had made sense, from the point of view of the United States at least, to take unilateral military action against Iraq, it made no sense at all for the United Kingdom to play so central and supporting a role in that unilateral action. It seems to us that the New Labour leader, in staying so close to the Bush Administration as it marched to war, boxed himself into a corner. It is a corner from which now he can only escape by claiming the status of either knave or fool. It is with the construction of that corner that the reflections in this chapter are centrally concerned.

New Territory

That we are in new territory now – put there by the events of 9/11 – cannot reasonably be denied. It certainly wasn't by Paul Wolfowitz when he appeared before the House and Senate Armed Services Committee within a month of the attacks. We face 'a new security environment', he told them, one in which 'surprise is back . . . the era of invulnerability is over' and 'our adversary has changed'.[1] When he was questioned on the origins of the Bush doctrine in a seminar at the International Institute for Strategic Studies in London in December 2002, he put it this way:

> I think that it goes back to some . . . understanding of just how profoundly the events of September 11th changed America's understanding of the risks and the stakes. I think indeed if we had understood that it was possible for 3,000 Americans to die in a single day, and ha[d] the graphic experience of what that entailed, we would probably have taken much more forceful action against Afghanistan long before. But we can't wait until 30,000 or even possibly 300,000 die as a result of an attack by weapons of mass destruction to deal with the threat posed by countries that have the weapons and develop them and support and work with terrorists. That is the heart of the issue . . . that instead of losing 3,000 people in a single day, it could be 10 or 100 or even 1,000 times as much, and that is not a threat we want to continue living with indefinitely.[2]

The new National Security Strategy document produced in September 2002 put it in similar terms.

> The nature of the Cold War threat required the United States – with our allies and friends – to emphasize deterrence of the enemy's use of force, producing a grim strategy of mutual assured destruction. With the collapse of the Soviet Union and the end of the Cold War, our security environment has undergone profound transformation . . . new deadly challenges have emerged . . . the United States can no longer rely on a reactive posture as we have in the past. The inability to deter a potential attacker, the immediacy of today's threats, and the magnitude of potential harm that could be caused by our adversaries' choice of weapons, does not permit that option. We cannot let our enemies strike first. . . . Traditional concepts of deterrence will not work against a terrorist enemy whose avowed tactics are wanton destruction and the targeting of innocents: whose so-called soldiers seek martyrdom in death and whose potent protection is statelessness.[3]

So far, so good: there is a new and potentially awesome danger, and it is one that is unresponsive to the old defence strategies of deterrence. Who can fault that? We certainly have no wish to do so. George Bush was quite right: 'now shadowy networks of individuals can bring great chaos and suffering to our shores for less than it costs to purchase a single tank.'[4] But the US analysis did not, and does not, stop there. Rather – and in the hands of all the leading figures in the Bush Administration – the argument is invariably pushed one stage further. It is embedded in a wider conceptual universe that includes 'rogue states' as well as 'terrorists'. This is a conceptual linkage that in its turn legitimates the focusing of American preventive action (often intentionally and sloppily termed 'pre-emptive' action[5]) onto those supporting 'rogue states'. 'To forestall or prevent such hostile acts by our adversaries', the National Security Strategy document declared, 'the United States will, if necessary, act preemptively'.[6] 'The greatest threat to freedom', Bush has become very fond of saying, 'lies at the crossroads of radicalism and technology.'[7] The USA might have difficulty in locating the radicals, but it can always bomb the technology. It can always go for the state as a surrogate for the networks that the state is said to support. The issue that we face, in the light of that, is whether 'bombing the technology', declaring a war on terrorism and forcing regime change in Iraq by military means provide the right and effective answer to the security problem posed by armed radicalism. We think that it does not: and in chapter 8 we will make the case for an alternative. For now it is sufficient to identify the overarching ethical and practical reasons why we think that, while the security threats are very real and serious, the war in Iraq as a response to them was profoundly wrong and counter-productive.

The Counter-Productive War

The first of these has to do with *honesty and integrity* in the design and implementation of foreign policy. If we are now into an era in which preventive war is one of the governing principles through which Great Powers relate to the rest of the world, then it is absolutely vital that the intelligence information on which the Great Powers design and implement counter-terrorist policies (whether genuinely pre-emptive or preventive) should be as solid as it is possible to make it, and that the interpretation of that data should not be overlayered by other concerns and motivations. This was visibly *not* so in this case. The evidence is now overwhelming that the Bush Administration put its own 'spin' on the tentative intelligence data coming to it, and that parallel, if more subdued, overselling of information then took place in London as a consequence. The prime 'criminals' here are in Washington. As Paul Krugman put it: 'there is no longer any serious doubt that Bush administration officials deceived us into war': all that is now in doubt is 'why so many influential people are in denial, unwilling to admit the obvious'.[8] The Krugman evidence, building on investigative journalism from the *Washington Post* and the *New Republic* as well as the *New York Times*, focused on the ambiguities and over-claims in George Bush's speech of 7 October – ironically titled 'Denial and Deception' – in which he left the distinct impression in the mind of the US electorate that the links between Saddam Hussein and bin Laden ran back over a decade, and were particularly strong.[9] But Krugman could equally have drawn on the Administration's failure clearly to dissociate itself from the discredited reports of the Iraqi hunt in Africa for components necessary for the construction of nuclear weapons, or on the embroidery of claims (about 45-minute delivery systems) in the first of the British dossiers on the Iraqi threat. As this book goes to print, standing committees in both the House of Commons and the Congress are providing chapter and verse on this oversell. And if the case was oversold, the issue at stake becomes 'why?' Was it because of the close connections between key Administration figures and companies with commercial interests in Iraqi oil, or Iraqi reconstruction? Was it because of unfinished business from the first Gulf War? Was it because of a long-term US need for a tame satellite in the Middle East? The very fact that the questions now have to be asked makes the point. The invasion of Iraq was not undertaken solely for the reasons publicly given by the politicians triggering it; and because it was not, any vestigial legitimacy that the invasion could glean from its links to the events of 9/11 are completely and totally eroded.

The second reason why the invasion of Iraq was not an appropriate response to the moral outrage felt in the United States after the events of 9/11 has everything to do with *blowback* from the role of previous US and UK governments in helping to create and sustain the regime that was now to be invaded. The attacks of 9/11 were themselves in part a product of blowback, if by blowback we understand a set of intelligible if hostile responses in one time period to policy pursued by a Great Power (in this instance, by the United States) in a previous time period. The attacks of 9/11 were a specific and extreme manifestation of the deep resentment felt by many people in many parts of the world against long-established aspects of US foreign policy, particularly US support for repressive regimes and US tolerance of steady and persistent Israeli refusals to implement UN resolutions requiring withdrawal from the territories occupied in 1967. To many Arab noses, US outrage against Hussein's refusal to honour UN resolutions had the unmistakable odour of hypocrisy about it, and that odour was only intensified by the growing evidence of previous active US and UK support for the Iraqi regime. The UK Government had financed the building of a key chemical plant. The United States had supplied the regime with weapons of mass destruction – chemical certainly, biological possibly – and in truth the UK's responsibility for the troubled politics of Iraq runs further back still, to the manner of Iraq's initial creation under British influence in the wake of the collapse of the Ottoman Empire. Here were major western powers bewailing the proliferation of lethal weaponry, yet at the same time actively selling other kinds of remarkably lethal weapons in export markets around the world.[10] Here were major western powers criticizing Hussein for using chemical agents in a war against his neighbour when simultaneously evidence was emerging of the far greater use of chemical weapons by the USA in an earlier war – Vietnam.[11] Here were western powers reacting with outrage and enlisting support for a military campaign to avenge the terror wrought on 11 September, and yet the USA had tolerated military coups in Indonesia in 1965 and in Chile in 1973 which operated through terrorism, resisted international mobilization to avert the terror of Rwandan genocide and supported the sanctions regime in Iraq which resulted in the death of untold thousands of Iraqi children. America might now suddenly have discovered the notion of a 'rogue state', but to many on the receiving end of US foreign policy in the Cold War era, the USA itself was, and had long been, a rogue state in its own right, doing all the things that rogue states do: funding terrorists, performing covert operations, undermining democratic governments, or tolerating and supporting those that did.[12] It was a bit late by 2003 for both the USA and UK to play the avenging angel. Avenging angels require clean hands, and neither the USA nor the UK had such hands by then.

In any event, invading Iraq in the name of an international community, the majority of whose members dissented from the operation, could only be – and is proving to be – entirely *counter-productive*. The intervention in Iraq, though presented as the next stage in the war on terrorism, has actually pulled resources away from that war, and enlarged the scope of the war to be fought. It is as though, having committed the USA to fighting both the perpetrators of terror and their supporters, the Bush Administration is finding it easier to fight their so-called supporters (namely Arab governments of a particular kind) than to fight the terrorist organizations themselves. But that strategy begs the question of whether, in the end, there is a military as distinct from a security solution to attacks of the al-Qaeda variety. There may be an internal security solution – the one of eternal vigilance – but is there an external military one? The general lesson (of both Vietnam and Northern Ireland) is that there is not.

Both these cases would suggest that foreign governments cannot suppress terrorist and guerrilla networks militarily. They can contain them by tight security, and that is undoubtedly a necessary thing to do once those networks have mobilized against a particular government or society. They can discourage failed states or predatory states from giving terror groups safe harbour; and indeed (as we will argue more fully in chapter 8) they should do so, if necessary, by using focused military engagements as part of a broader diplomatic, investigative and juridical strategy. But if the terrorist or guerrilla networks have popular support, they cannot be crushed without a level of state violence that destroys the very groups that the government is trying to win away from the terrorists. For if governments pre-emptively strike with overwhelming force at a terror network with already established social roots, then they simply act as its recruiting agent.

For that reason, the strategy of unilateral militarism was flawed in relation to Iraq itself. The speed and ease of the military victory should not deceive anyone into thinking that this victory is anything but pyrrhic. The very speed and character of the victory stands every chance of relegitimating al-Qaeda and its equivalents across the Arab world, so easing their problems of recruitment and finance; and the authorship of the victory leaves structures of global governance, weak before, now weaker still. Because they are, and because anti-American sentiment has been so strengthened across the entirety of the Middle East by the invasion,[13] it seems safe (though tragic) to predict that we now face the absolute guarantee of future attacks on the USA, and an associated cycle of 'attack, response, attack, response' for years to come. Invading Iraq in this manner has not brought widespread respect for US values and institutions – just the reverse. And to the extent that the Anglo-American invasion of Iraq has opened the road to a real Middle East settlement – an assertion that is, at best, premature at this stage – the regeneration of that peace settlement is not in any way dependent on the revitalization of Iraqi democracy, as Vice-President Cheney and others regularly claimed before the invasion that it was.[14] Imperial power and a huge and potentially permanent garrison of American military forces in the region are more than enough to buy photo-ops and lip-service support for the roadmap in Middle Eastern capitals from Tel Aviv to Damascus. But there is little likelihood that enduring peace can be purchased at this price, or that democracy across the region – in Saudi Arabia? in the Gulf Emirates? – can be established through war and occupation. More likely, as the French argued prior to the invasion, American policy in the Middle East will 'foster terrorism rather than . . . suppress it. The Americans have lit a match in a room full of gas', according to a French official cited in *The Economist*;[15] and the main social force likely to step into the political breach in Iraq created by the resulting blast will be the Shiite majority. The creation of a Shiite bloc running through Baghdad from Tehran to Damascus can hardly have been George Bush's long-term aim as the Anglo-American invasion began; but it may yet prove to be its major consequence.

Nor has the war in Iraq made the world in any obvious way safer for US and UK citizens. On the contrary, within a month of the war being officially 'won', suicide bombers struck in Saudi Arabia, Morocco and Israel; and the daily death toll among US troops (and by June 2003 even among UK troops) in Iraq has continued to grow. For what is clear is that, if western governments do want to isolate radical Islamic fundamentalism effectively, they have to strengthen – as Paul Wolfowitz himself regularly points out – voices of moderation in the Arab world; and military intervention will not do that. What is also clear is that the strengthening of moderation in the Arab world requires that the global community address the political, economic and social problems that generate popular support for radical Islamic forces in the first place. There is no quick military fix here. Nor is the rise of Islamic fundamentalism purely (or mainly) a theological phenomenon. It is a social one;[16] and because it is, the resources now deployed militarily, and the political will so focused upon them, need to be redirected with equal vigour to programmes of economic and social reconstruction. The answer to al-Qaeda requires security at home in the USA. That is certain. But it also requires, among other things, the creation of a viable Palestinian state, a democratized Saudi Arabia and a large Arabian and Muslim middle class in the Middle East sustained by prolonged economic growth. A determined effort to get the Israelis to remove settlements and cede control in the territories, and to get the Palestinian Authority to secure Israel against terror attacks, backed by a new Marshall Plan, would have been a better solution to the problems triggered by the events of 9/11 than any form of 'Operation Iraqi freedom'. But try telling that to the neo-conservative policy hawks so emboldened by the 'successful' invasion they have triggered!

The Blair Error

The presence of such conservative forces in the policy circles surrounding the Bush Administration only serves to illustrate how bizarre it is that so self-consciously a 'third way' UK Government should have allied itself so closely to the American cause. For governments to stand shoulder-to-shoulder requires the prior existence of a deep empathy of values between them. Standing shoulder-to-shoulder requires a commonality of world view. It suggests a oneness of interests and priorities. It works best if those standing together also stand, when alone, in broadly the same global position, with the same global status. But the UK and the USA are not like this. Tony Blair repeatedly asserted a set of shared values between London and Washington, and at the most general level that is undoubtedly so. Both governments are elected democracies, with a long history of close (if originally hostile) relationships. But there is, or should be, no proximity of values and world views between a party of the centre-left and the kind of Republicans now in command of both the White House and Congress. As the Republican National Committee put it in a fund-raising letter distributed as the war in Iraq raged, in the US political system 'a fierce battle is being waged at this very moment for the heart and soul of America . . . the liberals are retrenching!'[17] It is hard to capture in a single sentence the venality, parochialism and lack of genuine charity characteristic of the American Right. Perhaps it is enough to say that the natural allies of these political forces within the UK political system are the remnants of the Thatcherites, not the leaders of New Labour. It is Margaret Thatcher who still walks tall in the Republican pantheon, not Tony Blair. What values, we are obliged to ask, does New Labour share with a Republican leadership that, surrounded by political allies of an intensely right-wing hue, is hard-pressed to deliver even its own modest form of 'compassionate Conservatism'?

Nonetheless and in the wake of 9/11, Tony Blair seemed determined to create a proximity to George Bush that mirrored the closeness he had enjoyed earlier with the politically more empathetic Bill Clinton.[18] Indeed, it would not be too much to say that the re-creation of this personal and political closeness then itself became *the* object of UK policy. If the detail of Woodward's reporting is accurate, Blair really forced himself onto the Bush White House in September 2001: forced himself so much, in fact, that the senior Bush people didn't initially know quite what to make of him, or what to do with him.[19] And certainly later, when Blair hesitated in the move to war, Rumsfeld was quick to make clear that, though it was good to have the UK along for the ride, the USA was quite prepared to do the job in Iraq alone if Blair hadn't the bottle for the fight. It was problematic enough for the UK to stand close to the Washington political establishment in the late 1990s, when Democrats ran the White House; but did no one in the New Labour cabinet worry that, through his strong stance on Iraq, Tony Blair was fast becoming the favourite European political leader of people like Rumsfeld, Perle and Wolfowitz?[20] And did it not worry Tony Blair that the Bush Administration was – both privately and publicly – so committed to regime change in Baghdad that there was literally nothing that Saddam Hussein could do to lessen that commitment? Did Blair not see this? Or did he see it, and discount its importance? Or was he too, for all his public utterances to the contrary, prepared to see Saddam Hussein removed by force, even if the Iraqi regime voluntarily disarmed?

Questions such as these then raise the issue of what precisely is the relationship of interests between the USA and the UK. In the run-up to the war, Tony Blair and George Bush regularly announced that the relationship was a close one; but in reality, and even during the Clinton presidency, the interests of the USA and UK – though they overlapped in some general 'third way' sort of fashion – were still very different. For these differences were and are the product not just of the prevalence of different political philosophies in the two capitals, but also of differences in global position and standing. The USA is the last remaining global superpower. The UK, by contrast, is at most a former superpower now occupying a modest position as one of a number of leading Western European states. Administrations in the USA may feel the need to act alone. Multilateralism is, for them, a constraint on their unilateral freedom of action: and they are free to act alone. They have sufficient power to do so. They are not free to act alone without consequences, which is why multilateral forms of politics are still crucial to their foreign affairs, and why even the Bush Administration talks the language of coalition. But even then, in partnership or coalition, the USA expects to be the dominant force. Not so the UK: multilateralism in foreign affairs for second-order states of its standing is essential and empowering, not constraining. The UK has a real interest in enhancing the standing of supranational institutions, the rules of international law and the potency of the European Union as a global player. The USA does not. The USA has an electorate, significant sections of which revel in regular shows of force by its military abroad. The UK does not. UK governments that wish to avoid being merely the 'poodle' or the 'sidekick' of the American giant do not have the luxury of unilateralism. In an age in which the correct metaphor to describe US foreign policy is that of the American western – the self-confident law man chasing bandits, alone if he has to, with a posse if he can – the UK does itself no favours by being chief cheerleader for the posse.

New Labour possesses, as we have seen, the embryo of a new specification for UK foreign policy, and a distinct understanding of the social and economic origins of global violence. As we have seen too, Tony Blair chose, when under pressure from his domestic critics, to describe the Iraq invasion as a 'third way' war. But in truth it was not. Tony Blair took the UK to war in Iraq, in a military action that lacked general international support, only by retreating from the principles that were beginning to make the emerging New Labour foreign policy distinctive. He went back to an older set of foreign policy instincts – instincts that were pure Ernest Bevin – instincts of Atlanticism and the imperial use of UK military power. In his foreign policy towards Iraq, Tony Blair proved himself to be far more Old Labour than he characteristically likes to claim; and in so doing he demonstrated the residual impact on UK foreign policy of its imperial past. Imperial mindsets are morally unacceptable and globally dangerous wherever they occur – in Washington no less than in London – so in singling out Tony Blair here for censure, we have no wish to lessen our parallel condemnation of US imperialism. It just seems particularly unfortunate to us that in the UK case, having left its colonial past behind, the UK's political class should be finding it so difficult to shed the residues of the attitudes that once sustained the Empire. For in the way in which the New Labour Government felt it had the right to invade Iraq without a renewed UN mandate, we see again the quite staggering arrogance and self-absorption of the imperial power: the kind that makes it legitimate for UK troops to rearrange the political architecture of someone else's country, even though any similar attempt by foreign armies in the UK would be treated as a simple matter of aggression, legitimately to be repelled. We see again the quite staggering capacity for self-deception characteristic of imperialists: the kind that makes UK governments expect gratitude and support from those 'liberated', rather than resentment and resistance. If the speed and ease with which New Labour went to war in Iraq without a UN mandate make any one thing clear, it is this: that the intellectual furniture of Victorian imperialism still remains a presence in the mindset of the existing leadership of the Labour Party. It is a furniture that long ago should have been thrown out and burnt.

The ease with which Tony Blair dropped back into older foreign policy habits also points to a weakness that is modern as well as Victorian. New Labour prides itself on the intellectual coherence, as well as the moral underpinnings, of its modernizing strategies, both at home and abroad. Tony Blair has been quite comfortable playing the global advocate of third-wayism, just as, earlier, Margaret Thatcher was of her neo-liberal conservatism. Blair clearly thinks that he has a package to sell that will work for everyone. But the intellectual penetration of the third way analysis is extremely thin. If there is coherence, there is also superficiality. As we saw in chapter 6, there is superficiality in the analysis that is applied to the UK: a steadfast refusal to address the residual issues of class inequalities and residual imperial attitudes and practices that block any easy route to a broad-based growth-generating 'partnership' between capital and labour. There is superficiality of a similar kind in the analysis that is applied to the world of which the UK is a part: globalization is again understood as a set of broadly benign processes free of class and imperial contradictions. No New Labour leader will lecture the world on the legacies of combined but uneven development, and the inappropriateness of free trade to their resolution. Set against the world vision of New Labour – infused as it is with the same neo-liberal enthusiasm for open markets that animates the Bush Administration[21] – even the reports of the Brandt Commission of a generation ago look to be documents of immense radicalism.[22] Because they do, New Labour leaders are able, when they choose, to cherry-pick causes on which to moralize and act, as though each was available for resolution alone. At least the Bush Administration seems to be engaged in a coherent global imperial project in which all the pieces fit together, and in which bits (like Iraq) gather significance because of their place in the interstices of the whole. But New Labour leaps on and off that imperial project as the fancy takes it – getting excited about Iraq this year, and who knows about what next year. *Unanchored moralizing* of this kind is not only dangerous and self-defeating, though it is certainly both those things; it is also indicative of an inadequacy in theorizing and understanding. How else are we to explain the speed with which Tony Blair adopted what Rumsfeld called the new language – that of 'war', 'terrorism' and 'weapons of mass destruction' – except by noting that, prior to receiving this American linguistic leadership, New Labour lacked a rigorous conceptual apparatus of its own?

What seems to have happened to the New Labour Government as the events leading to the invasion of Iraq unfolded was that in part they became victims of their own prior statements. Having argued in Texas in April 2002 that there were certain regimes in the world that were too dangerous to be left in place, and that it was essential that the international community act to contain or remove them, by early 2003 Tony Blair had reached the moment he had long tried to postpone. He had reached the moment at which the dilemma written into the linkage he laid out in April could be avoided no longer – the moment, that is, when the condemned regimes were still in existence but the multilateral coalition to remove them was not. How then to jump? Had the status of the regime been changed by the absence of an international will to remove it? No, of course not. Was the regime too dangerous to leave in place? Blair was on record as saying so. So the case for unilateral action won, as it were, by default. Blair did not want to act without UN backing, but he couldn't get that backing; and he had argued himself into a corner in which inaction against the regimes being criticized was no longer a possibility. The logic of path dependency then took over.

This seems to us a more valuable way of understanding the drift to war than that of trying to determine the precise date on which Tony Blair took the decision. But we may be in a minority here. There are many of Tony Blair's critics who are convinced that he made up his mind to go to war sometime during 2002 – either in April or in September. Whether they are right or not will be an issue for the biographers. What seems to us more potent, and more pertinent, were the logics taking him to that decision, whenever precisely he took it: logics which, once in place, were extraordinarily hard to break. For these were logics that were so resilient that even when his chief of staff told those drafting the September 2002 dossier that 'we will need to make it clear in launching the document that we do not claim that we have evidence that [Saddam] is an imminent threat', Tony Blair still chose to make that launch by claiming that Saddam 'has existing and active military plans for the use of chemical and biological weapons which could be activated within 45 minutes'.[23] They were logics that were so resilient that, although senior intelligence figures warned him immediately prior to the invasion that military action against Iraq ran the risk of *increasing* the threat of terrorist attacks, he went ahead with the invasion nonetheless.[24] They were logics that he laid out for all to see when defending his decision before a sceptical party conference in 2003.

> I ask just one thing: attack my decision but at least understand why I took it and why I would take the same decision again. Imagine you are PM. And you receive this intelligence. And not just about Iraq. But about the whole murky trade in WMD [weapons of mass destruction]. And one thing we know. Not from intelligence. But from historical fact. That Saddam's regime has not just developed but used such weapons gassing thousands of his own people. And has lied about it consistently, concealing it for years even under the noses of the UN inspectors. And I see the terrorism and the trade in WMD growing. And I look at Saddam's country and I see its people in torment ground underfoot by his and his sons' brutality and wickedness. So what do I do? Say 'I've got the intelligence but I've a hunch it's wrong'? Leave Saddam in place but now with the world's democracies humiliated and him emboldened?

You see, I believe the security threat of the 21st century is not countries waging conventional war. I believe that in today's interdependent world the threat is chaos. It is fanaticism defeating reason. Suppose the terrorists repeated September 11th or worse. Suppose they got hold of a chemical or biological or nuclear dirty bomb; and if they could, they would. What then? And if this is the threat of the 21st century, Britain should be in there helping confront it, not because we are America's poodle, but because dealing with it will make Britain safer. There was no easy choice.[25]

Tony Blair took the UK to war alongside the United States in March 2003 because by his public statements he had locked the UK into a path of confrontation with Iraq, by standing alongside the USA in its condemnation of the Iraqi regime. It was not a path from which escape was then possible without loss of face, and without imperilling the relationship with the USA to which he had given unique priority and on which he was prepared to surrender New Labour's commitment to multilateralism and, if need be, his party's fortunes. Nor was it a path from which escape was possible without bolstering the self-confidence of the Iraqi regime that both the US and UK Governments claimed was so dangerous. So the UK went to war in a *comedy of errors*, locked into a sequence of events that its Government had worked so hard to avoid. This is fully in line with Robin Cook's suggestion, in his diaries published in October 2003, that by the time war became inevitable, Tony Blair was 'genuinely puzzled as to how he had got himself into his present dilemma'. It was Cook's judgement that Blair 'had never expected to find himself ordering British troops into war without UN backing', particularly given that by then – again in Cook's judgement – Blair did not believe any longer in the veracity of the claim, made in the September 2002 dossier, that Saddam Hussein had weapons of mass destruction that could be deployed within 45 minutes.[26] 'I am certain', Cook wrote, that 'the real reason he went to war was that he found it easier to resist the public opinion of Britain than he did the request of the President of the United States.'[27]

Comedies of errors of this kind can be avoided in the future, of course, by the early adoption of verbal restraint. They can be avoided, that is, if and to the degree that, whenever next the USA singles out a rogue state, UK ministers are more cautious in their opening statements. But similar 'comedies' (really tragedies of course) will occur nonetheless, unless UK governments in addition make a sharp break with the 'unique UK world role' arrogance inherited from the imperial period, the very arrogance indeed that led Tony Blair to put the UK on that US-specified path in the first place. The best way to avoid 'accidents' of the Iraqi war kind happening again, that is, is to make a sharp break with the mindset that generated this one.

Of course, those of us critical of the unilateral invasion of Iraq are now often ourselves criticized, by those who followed Tony Blair into that corner, for advocating a form of international inertia that would have left the repressive regime of Saddam Hussein in power.[28] That criticism is, however, entirely misplaced. Those critical of the invasion took the stance that they did because of the unilateral nature of the invasion, their mistrust of American and British motives, and their concern about the humanitarian catastrophe that war would bring, and not because of any willingness to acquiesce in Saddam Hussein's abominations. And those advocating the war have their own problem here in any case: the problem of timing. If the moral case for intervention was so strong in 2003, on virtually any recognizable moral criteria 'the moral case for invasion would have been stronger in 1988, when Saddam was gassing the Kurds, or in 1991, when he was slaughtering the Shia'.[29] But where was the war party then? And it is worth remembering that Tony Blair himself did not ground the case for going to war on the moral issue itself. The nature of the regime was a factor in his legitimation of intervention, but always a secondary one. This was the way he handled the issue before the Liaison Committee:

> Q169 MR BEITH You referred to the Saddam Hussein regime as 'an appalling regime the world was well rid of', and I doubt if there are many people who would disagree with you about that. Does that mean that we were powerless to do anything about it unless Saddam Hussein persisted in non-compliance?

> MR BLAIR That is a very good question. The truth is that to take action we had to have the proper legal basis and that was through the weapons of mass destruction issue and the non-compliance with the UN inspectors. What I have always said is that the relevance of the nature of the regime is that a regime that, say, was otherwise benign but had weapons of mass destruction you might take a different attitude to than a regime that was so savage and repressive and had weapons of mass destruction. I accept entirely the legal basis for action was through weapons of mass destruction.[30]

In any event, as Tony Blair himself said endlessly, there are just far too many repressive regimes (including among the countries that constituted the coalition of the willing) for the democratic part of the international community to take them all out by military force. The move against Iraq, as he said, was justified not because it was internally repressive, but because it constituted a potential and real external threat. Yet we now know that, in the pursuit of their imperial project, key members of the US Administration exaggerated the immediate threat posed by Saddam Hussein. We also now know that this exaggeration was recognized as such by the leaders of a string of western nations, and by the leaders of Russia, China and most developing countries as well. It was not, however, recognized in any public form by the leaders of New Labour. As the evidence mounted that the war was being oversold, time and again Labour supporters in the UK said to each other: 'Tony Blair must know something that he can't tell us, for reasons of intelligence and security' – but apparently he did not. All the New Labour leader had to guide him was the very intelligence information that is now being exposed as far more conditional and tentative than we were told prior to the invasion. So the question comes to this: did Tony Blair know that the data was problematic, but went on nonetheless, because having started on the Bush bandwagon, he could not get off without personal loss of face? Or did he not know? Was he actually bushwhacked, bamboozled by the overselling of the intelligence data by the Bush team? It is some choice. *The UK went to war when it should not have done so, led by a prime minister who was either misleading us or being misled himself.* Heaven forbid we should arrive at the next chapter of the Bush Administration's imperial saga with leadership in the UK as ill-equipped as this.

Towards an Ethical Foreign Policy

Thus far we have attempted to let the facts speak for themselves: to equip the reader with the information needed to make an informed assessment of the foreign policy that produced UK involvement in the invasion of Iraq. But of course in gathering that information we have formulated our own judgement that the policy pursued was woefully inadequate, and we have grown increasingly conscious of the need for a sharp break with the trajectory of that policy. We have come, that is, to our own understanding of what the New Labour Government needs now to do, if UK involvement in future 'wars with Iraq' is not to litter the decades to come.

What follows in this chapter, therefore, is our view of how the UK should recast its foreign policy to make the most of the lessons of this sorry episode and apply them to the implementation of a practical-minded yet progressive foreign policy. What has gone before in this volume is not conditional upon the content of what is now to follow, though what is now to follow is highly conditioned by the content of all that you have just read. It would not be right, in our view, to be critical of so important a policy stance without offering principles that underpin our preferred alternative; and it would not be right if those alternative principles were simply parachuted in at the end, presented without linkage back to what has gone before. So what follows here is our own interpretation, but that interpretation should come as no surprise. It grows from what we have established before; and it is offered, as this book as a whole is offered, as one contribution to the now vitally needed public debate in the UK on what New Labour's foreign policy should be in the next phase of its tenure of office.

In this chapter, we will move beyond the debate about why Tony Blair decided to make the UK fight in George Bush's war. In the context set by the competing ethical frameworks that have animated Old and New Labour foreign policy debates, we will develop a set of alternative ethical principles to guide a progressive foreign policy. We will begin from the recognition that whether in Iraq, the Middle East more generally, the Korean peninsula, West Africa, or wherever else Washington decides to direct its gaze, the American projection of power – instinctively unilateralist and unfailingly exercised on its own terms even when ad-hoc multilateralism prevails – dominates the foreign policy horizon. We will ask what options remain for the UK to advance its national interests and yet preserve a critical degree of independence from the American colossus; and we will explore the degree to which the British Labour Party can still rewrite its foreign policy in ways that draw on its historic socialist heritage and mission, integrate the domestic and foreign policy elements of its claim to government and bridge the gap between the perpetual demands for humanitarian intervention and the UK's finite capacity to intervene with real effect.

In order to address these questions and to offer an alternative foreign policy to that currently being pursued by Tony Blair, we will examine four of the key issues that lay behind the rush to war in Iraq:

- how to meet the security threats in the post-9/11 world;
- the role of the Security Council in authorizing the use of force;
- when and how to intervene militarily to advance humanitarian ends;
- the strategy of the preventive use of force.

Previous chapters have established that the necessary empirical claims associated with the justifications for this particular war were either fabricated, not proven, or provided an insufficient rationale for the invasion of Iraq. In short, the previous chapters established that the justifications used for the invasion of Iraq failed the *empirical* test. It is time now to move beyond the debate about the facts of the case for war – as important as this remains – to investigate the moral justifications for current foreign policy and to offer an alternative ethical framework for policy to come. It is time, that is, to subject the justifications for the invasion of Iraq to an *ethical* test in addition to an empirical one; and to use that testing to open the way to the specification of a new and more progressive foreign policy for the UK.

Achieving Effect in the post-9/11 World

Speaking about the need for conciliation with the United States, the philosopher and statesman Edmund Burke observed as long ago as 1775 that 'the use of force alone is but temporary. It may subdue for a moment, but it does not remove the necessity of subduing again: and a nation is not governed which is perpetually to be conquered.'[1] His was a timely reminder that in any sane foreign policy the use of force should be subordinate to – or at the least integrated with – a robust arsenal of economic, diplomatic, social, humanitarian and political initiatives; and what made that reminder even more timely here was that his views were reintroduced into the debate on the Iraqi war by none other than Admiral Sir Michael Boyce, Chief of Defence Staff (CDS), in a high-profile Royal United Services Institute (RUSI) annual CDS lecture on 18 December 2002.[2] Boyce's reflections offer us a first element in the construction of an alternative foreign policy for the post-Iraq UK, and as such are worth reproducing in some detail here.

Boyce is a thoughtful and outspoken military man, whose views are widely reported on both sides of the Atlantic and on various sides of the debate about the war in Iraq. As an insider's insider at the apex of the defence establishment, he is undoubtedly a reluctant participant in our effort to forge a left-wing and progressive alternative to British foreign and security policy; but this is a fact that makes his testimony all the more powerful for our purposes. In a 2001 lecture Boyce warned that 'broader operations into regions that threaten UK policy goals will force us to choose between unconditional support to the coalition, conditional support, and "red lines" or selective support – or indeed lack of support'.[3] He argued that the UK's perspectives on promoting regional as well as global stability have been 'distorted by the focus on fighting terrorism', and he urged the UK Government to consider 'whether we wish to follow the United States' single-minded aim to finish Osama bin Laden and al-Qaeda' or take the lead and play to 'the UK's particular strengths in facilitating the nation-building process'. He argued with regard to both terrorism and weapons of mass destruction that the UK should take the pragmatic view – that there is an acceptable level of threat that the world can live with – and that the real challenge is to eliminate terrorism and the threat of weapons of mass destruction as 'a force for strategic effect'. There can be no mistaking Boyce's concern, in that 2001 lecture, that the UK might become trapped rather unwillingly in a coalition of the willing and capable – 'tied' as he put it 'into politico-military campaigns that will last decades because of their diffuseness'.[4] 'The strategic risks are obvious', he said:

> [A] UK military footprint might broaden the pan-Islamic perception of invasion; variations in loss of consent between traditionally bellicose factions might lead to mission creep and the dangers of peace enforcement, loss of impartiality and perceived clientism; resources might be diverted from priority missions; we might have a reticent and inadequate transition by the UN, leading to an unattainable exit strategy or end-state; and all of this added together resulting in inevitable strategic failure and all that might entail.[5]

Throughout his post-9/11 commentaries, straddling the line of propriety for the Chief of Defence Staff, Boyce has made it very clear that extending an ill-defined war against terrorism is a perilous exercise at best. The proper British response to the transformed post-9/11 security context, he seemed to tell us, must locate the use of force in a bigger picture; and that in the rush to extend the counter-terror war to Iraq, the larger political questions and consequences have been neglected, and that the UK ought not to have walked lock-step with the USA. The military effect of a war on terrorism must inevitably be limited, he explained, even ephemeral, in the absence of any hard strategic thinking about what the UK has to offer to an American-led coalition; what strengths it possesses and conditions it should set; how the war on terrorism affects the UK's work with the UN, NATO and the EU; what the political process of nation-building requires; and what the red-lines and exit strategies must be. In beginning to develop principles to guide British foreign policy, we could do far worse than elaborate on two of Boyce's clearest observations.

Principle 1   Conditional support for unauthorized coalitions

Consider all support for coalitions of the willing to be conditional, subject to 'red-lines', selective support and the open possibility of withdrawal of support.

Principle 2   The effect of force is temporary and limited

Take the pragmatic view that there is an acceptable level of risk from terrorism and weapons of mass destruction with which the world must – and can – live. Design comprehensive military, social, humanitarian and political policies not to wholly eradicate terrorism and weapons of mass destruction, but rather to manage the risks effectively and eliminate them as threats with strategic force.

The Dangers of Going Alone

As we know only too well by now, the attacks of 9/11 did more than kill an enormous number of innocent people. They also ended America's sense of invulnerability to foreign attack, unleashing dark fears of unknown enemy forces, and they invited the near certainty of US reprisals against the perpetrators of this horrendous series of attacks. They also brought a new language into play in global politics. For, as we saw in chapter 3, after some initial fleeting references to *criminality*, the official rhetoric quickly shifted into the language of *war*. By 8.30 p.m. on the evening of 11 September, in his address to the nation, President Bush referred to 'evil acts' and 'mass murder'. In brief and memorable remarks intended to rally the American people and restore confidence abroad, the President firmly established the frame of reference for everything that would follow. He stated very clearly, 'we will make no distinction between the terrorist who committed these acts and those who harbor them'; and, in the climactic point of the address, just before a call for prayers for the grieving families, declared that, 'America and our friends and allies join with all those who want peace and security in the world, and we stand together to win the war against terrorism.'[6]

Moreover, and again as we saw in more detail in chapter 3, it soon became clear that for George Bush the term 'war' was not meant here to be understood as a metaphor – the war on terrorism was not simply to be a more decisive, sustained and aggressive version of a war on crime or a war on drugs. As American just war theorist, Michael Walzer, lamented shortly after the attacks, 'military action is what everybody wants to talk about – not the metaphor of war, but the real thing'. Walzer did not think that this abandonment of metaphor was at all desirable. On the contrary, he argued that before any real war should be contemplated, three elements of a metaphorical war must come first: 'intensive police work across national borders, an ideological campaign to engage all the arguments and excuses for terrorism and reject them, and a serious and sustained diplomatic effort'.[7] But of course the trigger to real war had by then already been cocked. British historian Michael Howard went even further, arguing that America's declaration of war on terrorism was 'a very natural but terrible and irrevocable error'. According to Howard, British experience demonstrated that many such 'wars' could be conducted effectively – in Ireland, Palestine, Cyprus and Malaya (the modern Malaysia) – under the rubric of 'emergencies'; but he expressed grave concern that a public declaration that America was at war was actually self-defeating, inspiring 'a psychosis that may be totally counter-productive for the objective being sought'. Real war, he argued, requires an identifiable, hostile adversary that looks as much as possible like a traditional state, while an effective campaign against transnational terror requires a very different set of sensibilities and skills: 'secrecy, intelligence, political sagacity, quiet ruthlessness, covert actions that remain covert, above all infinite patience'. In his view at least,

> [M]any people would have preferred a police operation conducted under the auspices of the United Nations on behalf of the international community as a whole, against a criminal conspiracy whose members should be hunted down and brought before an international court, where they would receive a fair trial and, if found guilty, be awarded an appropriate sentence.[8]

Understandably, however, in the immediate wake of 9/11 neither US policy-makers nor, it must said, the overwhelming majority of ordinary Americans, had any taste for a long, drawn out, police investigation followed by a juridical process that would, at best, turn bin Laden into Milošević. For such a process would have robbed America of a chance at quick and decisive revenge for the catastrophic terror attack, and deprived it of the chance to defend itself directly against a second Pearl Harbor. Understandably too, the vast majority of Americans considered the attacks an affront to the nation – how could they not? The attacks were also experienced as a devastating psychological assault that left a long trail of grief and unending anxiety about future attacks – and daily worry for many millions of ordinary citizens about the safety of friends and loved ones as they headed off each morning to pursue their routine activities. And as we have seen, American public opinion and political leadership in the wake of 9/11 were not prepared to be patient or to rely on others to take the fight to al-Qaeda for them – or even with them, if that support had any strings attached. For however welcome to ordinary Americans the outpouring of international support for the USA was after 9/11, for them this was an American show.[9] The attacks were attacks against America. The question on everyone's lips was 'Why do they hate us?' They did not say: 'If only we had been able to complete the United Nations Comprehensive Convention on International Terrorism in time.'

Yet, in truth, the events of 11 September were unique among acts of terrorism in not being simply one country's 'show'. They included among those killed the citizens of dozens of countries and the consequences reverberated across the world; and because they did, the terrorist attacks of 9/11 required a unique – and uniquely collective – response. As one observer noted:

> [T]he attacks on New York and Washington . . . are different from those that have plagued London, Belfast, Madrid, and Moscow. Those unlawful acts were designed to change a particular policy, but not destroy a social organization. The ambition, scope, and intended fallout of the acts of September 11 make them an aggression, initially targeting the United States but aimed, through these and subsequent acts, at destroying the social and economic structures and values of a system of world public order, along with the international law that sustains it.[10]

It is understandable that Americans took the attacks of 9/11 personally, instantly and unilaterally declared a real and not merely a metaphorical war on terrorism, declined NATO's offer to give effect to its commitment to collective self-defence and categorically failed to recognize any formal authority of the Security Council regarding the use of force.[11] Understandable – but counter-productive. In our judgement, the first mistake that the UK Government made was to acquiesce this US position, if for no other reason than that the successful prosecution of the campaign against international terrorists begged for a robust exercise in *collective* and not unilateral self-defence.

The successful prosecution of a counter-terror campaign required – and continues to require – the level and scope of participation by countries throughout the world that is only possible with the formal institutional backing of the United Nations as well as of other key global and regional organizations. It also requires, as Walzer suggests, the mobilization of an alliance to engage and discredit all arguments and justifications for terrorism. Equally importantly, homeland security (even in the United States) will be as temporary in effect as the use of force itself until the motives for terrorism are exposed and its causes addressed. As Tariq Modood observed shortly after 9/11, 'our security in the West, no less than that of any other part of the world, depends upon being tough on the causes of terrorism, as well as terror itself'.[12] But of course, a shooting war crowds out such a reflective exercise; and a country that believes its president when he says that 'America was targeted for attack because we're the brightest beacon for freedom and opportunity in the world',[13] will not be able to discover the root causes of the terrorism directed against it – including, as these do, imperial arrogance, a history of military aggression, support for authoritarian regimes among allies in the Middle East and elsewhere, and complicity in a devastating global development gap.

In our judgement, the unilateral rhetorical declaration of a real military 'war on terrorism' by the United States after 9/11 should have been resisted by the UK and by other leading members of the international community. They should have insisted instead on the design and implementation of a multilateral and multifaceted counter-terrorist strategy that rejected a rhetorical declaration of war in favour of other things: an emphasis on protection from attack, a focused use of force to disrupt and disable terror groups and to discourage countries from providing safe harbour, and the prevention of future terror attacks by toughness on the causes of terrorism – and tough-mindedness in asserting that terrorism can have no moral justification whatever the claims.[14] All that is embodied here as Principle 3.

Principle 3 Security requires a coordinated campaign including the use of force but not a war on terrorism

Cross-border terrorism employed for strategic effect should be recognized as a fundamental assault on every member of the international community. It is a profound challenge to the system of collective security established by the UN Charter and should be met accordingly, through a multifaceted strategic mobilization at the level of regional and international organizations, including ideological, political, diplomatic, investigative, judicial and military dimensions. All acts of terrorism cannot be prevented, but their effect and frequency can best be contained in this manner. The remedy is not less force than a 'war on terrorism' implies, but the more effective, differentiated and integrated use of clearly defined, limited and, where possible, authorized use of force as 'a force for good' to disrupt and disable terror groups and deter states from harbouring them.

Meeting the Security Threat, Authorizing the Use of Force

Multilateral responses and exercises in collective self-defence against acts of terrorism require strong and effective international institutions for their creation and implementation; which is why, once it became clear that the United States was unalterably determined to wage a war on terrorism on its own terms, it was obvious too that the UN Charter system on the use of force faced a defining moment. An impending crisis for the Security Council, the United Nations and

the role of international law was clearly on the horizon. Legal schol-
ars were quick to worry that the use of the word 'war' to characterize
the response to the attacks of 9/11 could 'be manipulated to provide
an escape route from the constraints of international law'.[15] Faced
with such a set of options, many on the left have simply spoken out
against the use of force by the USA, without addressing the threat
posed by international terrorism; and others have insisted on a reading of international law that would make effective responses impossible. Neither of those responses seems satisfactory to us. Nor equally
would it be satisfactory in our view simply to offload responsibility
for the orchestration of a collective response to acts of terrorism onto
the UN in its present form. For given what we know about the Security Council – that its agenda is invariably controlled by the self-
interested machinations of the permanent five veto-wielding powers,
that it operates inconsistently, that it fails to enforce its own resolutions, and sometimes neglects or even violates international law, that
it is western-dominated, and that it is unable to resolve the problems
of selectivity and double-standards[16] – we can have little confidence
that ethical principles will guide decisions there. How then can we
begin to shape an ethical approach to the use of force in international
affairs?

We can begin by recognizing those flaws, and their institutional
and geopolitical origins and constraints, and by seeing that the changing nature of those constraints might yet offer a window of opportunity for change. As Niel Blokker has argued: 'From the outset, the
UN collective security system not only lacked the teeth of a standing
UN force, but in addition the Cold War prevented the Security Council
more generally from playing the role foreseen by the UN Charter.'[17]
Since the end of the Cold War, however, agreement among the five
permanent Security Council members has been easier to achieve: to
paradoxical effect. On the one hand, with the prospect of consensus has
come the revitalization of the Security Council's capacity and willingness to authorize what has come to be called 'delegated enforcement
action' (or more cynically the subcontracting or privatization of military enforcement actions). We have seen this on several important
occasions since 1990: in Iraq in the first Gulf War, and in the former
Yugoslavia, Somalia, Haiti, Sierra Leone, Guinea-Bissau and East
Timor. In fact, UN action of this kind has become quite routine. On
the other hand, as Blokker also noted, 'it is also clear that the role
which is in fact now being played by the Council is limited to legitimizing the use of force, without keeping it under strict control'.[18]

Without Security Council reform and in the absence of agreement over international rules to govern military intervention for

humanitarian purposes, the subject of humanitarian intervention has been very divisive. In Britain and elsewhere (mainly in the West) some on the left have fervently embraced intervention on human rights or humanitarian grounds. Others, principally from the developing world, have defiantly upheld the sovereignty of target states and rejected any right to intervene on the part of Great Powers as nothing more than a neo-imperialist throwback to the era of the civilizing missions of colonial powers. For several years, Secretary-General Kofi Annan has worked hard to break the deadlock and shift the terms of debate in an effort to build a consensus in favour of agreed principles for intervention – principles that would enhance the authority of the Security Council and improve the prospects of unified effective action in the face of imminent humanitarian catastrophe.

The most far-reaching effort thus far has been achieved by the International Commission on Intervention and State Sovereignty (ICISS), which was sponsored by the Canadian Government and reported to the Secretary-General in December 2001. The report helped establish a new language about humanitarian intervention – the 're-sponsibility to protect' – that has inspired new thinking in UN, NGO and diplomatic circles. In these terms, the responsibility to protect citizens from human rights abuses and other humanitarian crises replaces the capacity to control affairs within a defined territory as the cornerstone of sovereignty. If this responsibility to protect is not met, then it must (under very strict threshold criteria) be taken up by the international community. Will this new perspective on humanitarian intervention break the deadlock? It is too early to say, but not too early to observe that there is vigorous and quite productive debate under way in and around the United Nations in a race against time to create consensus and heal the divisions over the authorized and collective use of force before too many more Rwandas, Kosovos and Iraqs embroil international politics and erode the effectiveness of the Security Council.[19]

Understood in this way, the role of the Security Council, both actual and potential, in the war in Iraq and beyond, comes into clearer focus. When President Bush spoke to the General Assembly on 12 September 2002, he challenged the body to 'serve the purpose of its founding or become irrelevant'. As Richard Falk has noted, the war in Iraq left in its wake at least two answers to Bush's challenge. To the US Government, the failure to rubber-stamp the American and British decision to go to war ratified the irrelevance of the UN; but to those who opposed the war, the Security Council 'served the purpose of its founding by its refusal to endorse recourse to a war that could not be persuasively reconciled with the UN Charter and international law'.[20] We would offer a third response, namely that the diplomatic debacle at the UN before the war, and the manifest problems of securing order and rebuilding Iraq under the aegis of Anglo-American occupation after the war, create an opportunity for the Security Council to build on – and radically reform – its recent practice of legitimizing the delegated use of force. The scene is set for the Security Council – led by dissidents among the permanent five Security Council members as well as by rotating members – to insist that the Council exert greater control over the 'subcontracted' use of force in a manner that builds on the framework of the highly regarded ICISS approach.

Clearly, the Secretary-General is pressing such a reform agenda at every opportunity, most visibly in his presentation to open the United Nations General Assembly on 23 September 2003. In his much anticipated remarks, Annan acknowledged disagreements among member states about how to respond to the very real threats of terrorism and weapons of mass destruction. Then, in the heart of what has been called his most important speech as Secretary-General, Annan indirectly but unmistakably reproached the United States for its assertion that terrorism and the danger of weapons of mass destruction grant states 'the right and obligation to use force pre-emptively'. Annan expressed concern that if such a doctrine were accepted it could 'set precedents that resulted in a proliferation of the unilateral and lawless use of force, with or without justification'.

Rising to the occasion, despite his evident displeasure at the lawlessness of the Iraqi invasion, Annan gave credence to the underlying concerns that provided the impetus for the war in Iraq. It 'is not enough', he said, 'to denounce unilateralism, unless we face up squarely to the concerns that make some states feel uniquely vulnerable, since it is those concerns that drive them to take unilateral action.' 'We must show that those concerns can, and will, be addressed effectively through collective action.'[21] In other words, it is imperative that the Security Council urgently take up the necessary reforms that would obviate the need for states to act 'pre-emptively' to meet the threats such as those posed by terror networks with weapons of mass destruction – or by threats of the more traditional yet equally horrifying kind posed by ethnic cleansing or other massive human rights abuses.

We agree with Kofi Annan's sense of urgency about Security Council reform and with his effort to find a way to reconcile rapid response capabilities with collective authority, but we do not wish to appear naive here. We realize well enough that, given the existing structure of the Security Council and the cynicism of the present United States

Administration, balance of power realpolitik will continue to triumph over the classic principles of collective security enshrined in the Charter.[22] And we realize too that, even if the militarist proclivities of the USA and its capacity to enlist the UK in aggressive wars do abate, foreign policy will still have to operate in a world in which effective and legitimate global institutions are lacking – and yet in which predatory states and terror states are very much present. We will see that, under these circumstances, 'it may sometimes be necessary for non-predatory states to act unilaterally or outside the official institutional structure'.[23] That is not ideal from an ethical point of view, but it is inevitable nonetheless.

So under these highly imperfect conditions, what is the best we can hope for? First, we can hope that more sharply delineated conditions on delegated enforcement will serve as a reasonably effective bulwark against indiscriminate unilateral action. Second, closing the loopholes in delegated enforcement actions could significantly reform – and, in time, transform – the Security Council, and lend the United Nations greater effectiveness and authority on matters of use of force. Finally, even if – as is presently likely – the United States refuses to seek Security Council authority for the use of force, all will not be lost. For to the extent that other states reject the use of force without authority delegated by the Security Council and, at the same time, insist that the Security Council properly discharges its responsibility when faced with what the ICISS termed 'conscience-shocking situations crying out for action', the UN Charter system will be preserved. In this context of renewed focus on the responsibilities to protect citizens within a collective framework, we can reasonably hope that the fallout from the transparent Anglo-American abuse of the Security Council in the prelude to the war in Iraq will lead to a backlash of a particularly productive kind: a backlash expressed in a growing commitment by other states to apply strict conditions on enforcement actions. A developing consensus along these lines would, in our view, dramatically limit the use of force by states other than the USA. It would also shift global attitudes against the unilateral use of force by the USA itself, embolden and strengthen opponents and – we hope – reduce the future prospect of the UK Government embracing an increasingly lonely American assertion that unilateral might makes right.[24]

What might such an enhanced delegated enforcement model have looked like in the present crisis, and what might it look like in crises to come? As Robert Keohane has argued, the 'blank check' now written by the Security Council in authorizing states to use force would have been replaced by explicit agreements between the leaders of the coalition – in this case Blair and Bush and the Security Council – about the specific threats that justify the use of force, the political objectives of the military campaign, the conduct of the war and the treatment of civilians, and the responsibilities and mechanisms for the post-war occupation. As Keohane has rightly noted, the USA and UK would in those circumstances have been required before the war to answer some tough questions. Would they limit their wartime objectives to those authorized by the United Nations? After the war, would they use the resources they now controlled in Iraq only for purposes agreed to by the UN? Would they accept that the resources not be used to offset the costs of the war or to enhance American (and, we would add, British) power in the region? In addition, Keohane contended that under such a strengthened UN system, prior authorization would have been contingent on the acceptance, by both the US and UK Governments, of a set of benchmarks. These would have included: the immediate post-war access to Iraq by UN inspectors; compliance with all relevant international conventions and acceptance of responsibility, including financial claims, for their violation; acceptance of UN authority, after a very short time, over the use of the economic resources of the conquered country; and a commitment to the rapid turnover of authority to a UN administration, with civil authority over the country, supported for as long as necessary by forces from the occupying powers.[25]

We realize that prior authorization and an agreement on benchmarks such as these do not constitute the best of all possible worlds, since they tend to reinforce the trend toward authorized coalitions of the willing. We know full well that under these conditions enforcement actions are likely to be driven by the self-serving agendas of dominant powers, which can and will make every effort to intimidate Council members and threaten to act without authority if their conditions are not met. And, as we have seen so dramatically in the run-up to the war in Iraq, Security Council diplomacy can be dripping with hypocrisy, and may be held hostage to domestic politics on all sides. Which is why it is to be hoped that over time a standing force operating under the authority of the Security Council and the Secretary-General will be created; and that such a force, subject to strict conditions of prior authorization, will replace the 'subcontracting plus' approach outlined here. But we must search for ethical and sensible principles to govern conduct in the short term and in a radically imperfect world, where international affairs operate in a context of woefully inadequate institutions for global governance, endemic threats to security and a rule of law that is no more effective than the dominant international players permit it to be. In this grim context, we agree with Chris Brown that 'states should, as far as possible, try to act in such a way that they encourage the transformation of the world into one in which effective institutions do exist, or at a minimum do not make such a transformation more difficult'.[26]

Measured against this standard, we believe that the argument for transparently negotiated terms for prior authorization of delegated use of force holds the best prospect for mutually reinforcing successes. Both the credibility of the coalition and that of the UN Charter would be enhanced by this process and, at the same time, the broadest possible legitimacy and material support for the complex tasks of post-war reconstruction, democratization and nation-building would be assured. Hence our advocacy of Principle 4.

Principle 4   Reform the Security Council and enhance its authority to delegate the use of force based on prior authorization and benchmarks

The Security Council is deeply flawed and should be reformed to ensure greater consistency, transparency and equal-handedness in the execution of its responsibility – and to loosen its dependence on western powers which predominate among the permanent members and largely control the Council's agenda. Citizen groups and member states should work vigorously to reform the Security Council and to preserve and deepen its role in authorizing the use of force, ultimately by extending its capacity to advance collective security through the creation of a standing UN force. In the short term, in the absence of a standing force, member states can be expected themselves to initiate the use of force in crisis situations. Under these conditions, an ethical approach to the use of force – and one which at the same time carries the greatest hope of success because it provides the greatest legitimacy and mobilizes the widest and deepest support – requires explicitly negotiated, publicly debated and formally agreed prior authorization for the delegated use of force with clear justifications, insists on conditions and benchmarks for the conduct of military intervention as well as post-war reconstruction and nation-building. This reform would have the added benefit of advancing the very productive discussions initiated by the Secretary-General and advanced by the ICISS 'responsibility to protect' approach.

The prioritizing of honest and honourable efforts to secure delegated, stipulated authorization from the Security Council remains for us the mandatory precondition for the legal, just and effective use of force to respond to the security threats of the post-9/11 world. Anchoring this proposition is our firm belief that reliance on multilateral action, authorized and controlled by the United Nations, is not an ideological preference or merely one among a set of alternative options, but is something more. It is the only sensible long-term response to the recognition, to quote Jürgen Habermas's observation on the recent efforts to control Iraq by the unilateral exercise of military power, that 'a state that sees all its options reduced to the stupid alternatives of war or peace quickly runs up against the limits of its own organizational capacities. . . . It also steers the process of political and cultural negotiation down a false track, and drives the costs of coordination to dizzying heights':[27] hence Principle 5.

Principle 5   *Transfer of power and subsidiarity*

There is little cause for optimism that democracy and stability can be installed by force, certainly not in multi-ethnic societies, but the odds are improved by a delegated use of force which stipulates justifications for its use, compliance with international conventions that protect combatants and non-combatants, quickly transfers political and administrative authority to the United Nations – or, where possible, regional organizations – and mandates a rapid transfer of full authority to the United Nations or another multilateral organization. The principle of subsidiarity, that authority and responsibilities should be located at the lowest effective level possible, should be observed, since it holds the greatest chance of success in mobilizing support on the ground and resolving the extraordinarily difficult problems of cultural negotiation.

Justifications for Humanitarian Intervention

We realize of course that humanitarian intervention is always and invariably controversial, provoking profound questions that almost defy consistent universally applicable answers; and yet we are compelled to address a question at the heart of the debate about the war in Iraq. 'The mass graves, the underground dungeons, and the testimony of the tortured all leave no doubt about the criminal nature of the regime', wrote Habermas in raising the question of whether good consequences justify the use of force in Iraq after the fact. 'The liberation of a brutalized population from a barbaric regime is a greatest good; among political goods it is the greatest of all.'[28] Whatever the motives, deceptions, imperial designs and self-interested power plays of Bush and Blair, does the removal of the Saddam Hussein regime and the potential consolidation of a democratic, multi-ethnic, federal republic in Iraq justify the war on humanitarian grounds?

The politics of the Security Council – and, in particular, the risk of indefensible vetoes as in the Kosovo case – make it, in our view, impossible to rule out all use of force in the absence of Security Council blessings. We accept, with the Independent International Commission on Kosovo, that the intervention in Kosovo was 'illegal, but legitimate'. And there may be other such cases. It seems reasonable to consider on a case-by-case basis whether the decision of the Security Council passes muster in ethical terms, what benefits resulted from the intervention, and whether the authorization of another international body helps legitimate the use of force, despite the dangers associated with intervention that takes place without Security Council endorsement.[29] After all, increasing international support has been forthcoming lately for the principle that the need to intervene to prevent ethnic cleansing and other gross human rights catastrophes should trump the traditional rights of a sovereign state to assert exclusive jurisdiction and control over anything that occurs inside its borders. Indeed, since the 1990s, there has been an increasing trend to diminish the territorial authority of states when the international community sees fit to intervene in internal conflicts when human rights are profoundly jeopardized. This development, which advances a powerful ethical claim, has received significant support from the last three Secretaries-General. In fact, there is a growing consensus among international grassroots organizations and a widening circle of governments that the United Nations should act aggressively to initiate and support genuinely humanitarian intervention. (We need to remember that the UN was attacked for inconsistency and for doing too little, too late, to prevent catastrophic violations of human rights in places such as Bosnia and Rwanda, rather than for doing too much.[30]) This seismic shift in sensibilities and international norms was affirmed by UNSCR 1244 adopted in June 1999, which created a UN civil administration in Kosovo and imposed a peace treaty on Yugoslavia.[31] The stakes here are therefore very high. If the prior knowledge of ethnic cleansing justified intervention in Kosovo, despite the absence of authorization by the Security Council – and we think that it did – did prior knowledge of the heinous crimes of the Saddam Hussein regime justify the war in Iraq?

We answer bluntly that humanitarian intervention was justified in the Iraqi as in the Kosovo case, but not in the form of the Anglo-American war in Iraq. For when military intervention is undertaken for what are claimed to be humanitarian purposes outside the authority of the United Nations, it is our view that advocates of such action must meet a strong burden of proof set within a demanding framework of factual and procedural requirements.[32] First, evidence of grave, extensive human rights violations, perpetrated for strategic political purpose, must be established as a condition of proof. Second, there must be an exhaustion of all remedies short of war, including political initiatives, negotiations, inspection regimes and sanctions. Third, the case must be persuasively made for a humanitarian justification for the use of force: that the intervention contemplated is exclusively focused on humanitarian, rather than economic or strategic, aims.[33] Fourth, the control of a disinterested multilateral institution over the conduct of the intervention and an effective plan for post-war transfer of powers – in accordance with Principles 4 and 5 discussed above – must be established.

The case for Kosovo remains controversial, particularly as regards the relationship between the timing of the NATO campaign and the satisfaction of these requisite elements of proof. It was certainly an imperfect case for humanitarian intervention. Nevertheless, taken together, the evidence and threat of human rights catastrophes and the seriousness of the humanitarian justification for the use of force established key elements of the case for intervention, and the express UN mandate for a civil administration, after the fact, also helped to sustain the burden of proof. Yet, by contrast, the more we examine the criteria needed to meet the burden of proof for the invasion of Iraq, the more troubling the war in Iraq becomes. The mass graves are proof enough of the horrendous violations of human rights, and there can be no doubt that strategic aims anchored Saddam Hussein's brutality. No credible case, however, can be made for any of the other three elements needed to justify humanitarian intervention in Iraq. Had these conditions been met – or even nearly met – there would have been every reason to support humanitarian intervention in Iraq, but then the intervention that would have come would not have been a war designed in the back rooms of America's defence establishment to advance its own hegemonic designs. It would have been a genuine humanitarian intervention with limited and authorized use of force, within the spirit of 'the responsibility to protect', and subject to UN control and the rapid post-intervention transfer of authority. The invasion of Iraq was nothing of the kind, despite efforts by Tony Blair to maintain that it was.

According to press reports in the UK and Canada, as well as the testimony of UN insiders, after the war Tony Blair tried to stretch the 'responsibility to protect' doctrine to cover the case of Iraq – and who knows where else – by asserting that 'international responsibility to protect' trumps the principle of non-intervention, without specifying clear threshold conditions or binding obligations to seek UN authority. Blair was rebuffed in this effort at retroactive justification for war at the London summit of progressive world leaders last July and rightly so, for others present knew full well that the ICISS report was part of an effort both to enhance the sovereign capacity of states to protect their own citizens and to 'improve the capacity of the international community to react decisively' to gross and systematic violations of human rights. And they knew that the war in Iraq, rather than reconciling these two goals, torpedoed both. In fact, the Progressive Governance Summit formally stated in its communiqué: 'We are clear that the UN Security Council remains the sole body to authorize global action in dealing with humanitarian crises.'[34] No appeal to a right of humanitarian intervention can justify unilateral invasion: hence our sixth principle.

Principle 6   The justification for humanitarian intervention

Outside of the formal mandate of the UN Charter system, the burden of persuasion to justify humanitarian intervention must be very high, lest it be used as a convenient excuse for powerful states to advance their interests at the expense of less powerful states. Proof of imminent or ongoing humanitarian catastrophe must be established as the necessary but not the sufficient basis for justification. States contemplating military intervention for humanitarian purposes must persuasively argue that humanitarian aims – and not economic or geopolitical advantage – are the sole basis for the contemplated action. Relevant regional and international organizations must exhaust all remedies short of war. And the intervening states must subject their action to the control of an appropriate multilateral institution and agree to arrangements for the rapid transfer of civilian authority to it once order has been established and the humanitarian crisis resolved.

The Responsibility to Intervene

It is worth adding a point about humanitarian intervention that is often overlooked, particularly now in the aftermath of the Anglo-American skulduggery over Iraq, their manipulation of the Security Council and their flawed application of the concept of humanitarian intervention. The point is that the principles that should govern humanitarian intervention cut both ways. When the conditions are lacking, they should function as a constraint on intervention; but it is every bit as important to insist that when these conditions are met, the Security Council has a positive responsibility to authorize humanitarian intervention on the recommendation of the Secretary-General. Great Powers would then share that positive responsibility to intervene through delegated enforcement actions – as, on occasion, recently some of them have recognized. So the UK used military force to advance humanitarian ends and help stabilize Sierra Leone in 2000, as did France in the Ivory Coast in 2002. In both cases, permanent members took on responsibilities for the use of force to advance humanitarian intervention in their former colonies, in support of United Nations initiatives.

It is unfortunately true that the humanitarian demand for intervention exceeds the available supply of suitable interveners, and that Tony Blair is right to worry about the 'danger of letting wherever CNN roves be the cattle prod to take a global conflict seriously'.[35] But in our view such considerations do not excuse inertia in the face of catastrophic violations of human rights for political purpose, especially where there are historic ties that inspire greater responsibility – as in Sierra Leone, the Ivory Coast and now Liberia. In Liberia, settled in the nineteenth century by freed black slaves from the United States, America has a profound historical and moral responsibility to intervene and break the cycle of political violence and attempt to stabilize the country. Hundreds of thousands have been killed there of late, caught in the crossfire of warring factions that began in 1980. Yet Secretary of Defense Rumsfeld reportedly balked at sending US forces, saying they were overextended and, more to the point, that Liberia is not a vital American interest. The duration and scale of the US intervention suggest that Rumsfeld's view held sway. Of the roughly 3,000 American military personnel positioned on two amphibious assault ships off Liberia's coast, the vast majority never set foot on Liberian soil – and many who did were used to protect the US embassy in Morovia. A few hundred assisted West African peacekeepers in mid-August 2003 for less than two weeks, and a handful more moved back and forth between ship and shore in September. The claim that humanitarian intervention should only be contemplated when 'national interests' are at stake is not, in our view, an acceptable argument for non-intervention. On the contrary, when military intervention is clearly in the vital national interests of economic and geopolitical gain, that is when we have the problem of imperial overreach thinly veiled as humanitarian intervention. Humanitarian intervention is only credible, in our view, when 'vital interests' are absent. Hence Principle 7.

Principle 7   *The responsibility to intervene*

The doctrine and practice of humanitarian intervention includes not only prohibitions against unjustified intervention, but also positive responsibility for the Security Council to authorize and for powerful states to undertake enforcement actions to prevent or contain gross politically motivated violations of human rights. When the necessary conditions are met – proof, exhaustion of all remedies short of war, humanitarian justification for the use of force, and the control of a disinterested multilateral institution – the responsibility to intervene should be discharged by states connected to the target states by colonial histories or similar morally significant ties so long as they are willing to operate under strict stipulated authority.

Pre-emptive and Preventive Wars

In theories of just war and in international law, as in common sense, we find reference to the notion of *pre-emptive war* (a necessity of self-defence 'like a reflex action, a throwing up of one's arms at the very last minute') and to that of *preventive war* (an option based on strategic clairvoyance, 'an attack that responds to a distant danger, a matter of foresight and free choice').[36] This distinction is of vital importance here, because Iraq has just been the subject of a preventive war pretending to be a pre-emptive one.

Despite George Bush's effort to paper over the distinction between pre-emptive and preventive war, it must be recognized. There remains a huge chasm between the two versions of anticipatory military engagement. It was a chasm that Tony Blair should have recognized, given that in the UK's own post-9/11 strategic defence review prevention was defined quite differently – as conflict prevention focused on finding the root causes of terrorism, preventing instability and engaging actively in 'defence diplomacy'.[37] For, as Richard Betts has rightly observed:

> Pre-emption is unobjectionable in principle, since it is only an act of anticipatory self-defense in a war effectively initiated by the enemy. If the term is used accurately, rather than in the sloppy or disingenuous manner in which the Bush administration has used it to justify preventive war against Iraq, pre-emption assumes detection of enemy mobilization of forces to attack, which represents the start of war.[38]

It should be clear by now that no such claim was ever made by George Bush or Tony Blair. Instead we find a vaguely argued claim – initially tested by George Bush in his West Point graduation speech in June 2002[39] and subsequently formalized in the National Security Strategy issued in September 2002[40] – that new dangers at the 'crossroads of radicalism and technology' require a new strategic posture. The National Security Strategy document in effect sought to justify the prioritizing of preventive action by the United States by asserting that the events of 9/11 created a particularly grave threat that could not be met by the traditional Cold War doctrines of containment and deterrence: 'We must be prepared to stop rogue states and their terrorist clients', it said, 'before they are able to threaten or use weapons of mass destruction against the United States and our allies and friends.'[41] Yet buried within the Strategy document was an argument for preventive wars that wasn't new at all: the classic realpolitik rationale for preventive war that has far less to do with the real concerns of post-9/11 security and far more to do with America's assertion of a Manifest Destiny to lock in the advantages of overwhelming and irresistible power. Consider this excerpt from the National Security Strategy document.

> The United States must and will maintain the capability to defeat any attempt by an enemy – whether a state or non-state actor – to impose its will on the United States, our allies, or our friends. . . . Our forces will be strong enough to dissuade potential adversaries from pursuing a military build-up in hopes of surpassing, or equaling, the power of the United States.[42]

Michael Walzer has argued convincingly that preventive war assumes a 'standard against which danger is to be measured' that has nothing to do with the facts on the ground, 'but exists in the mind's eye, in the idea of a balance of power' which has become the dominant idea in international relations for 300 years or more: that in truth 'a preventive war is a war fought to maintain the balance of power'.[43] For that reason among others, we agree with Richard Betts that 'preventive war is almost always a bad choice, strategically as well as morally',[44] not least because, in moral terms, preventive war is never justified in the absence of what Walzer calls '*just fear*'[45] – and that condition is nearly always lacking in preventive as distinct from pre-emptive wars. It certainly was lacking in the case of the war in Iraq. For this was not even an adequately anchored preventive war. It had less in common with the serious prevention of a future danger than it had with those potty schemes of cabals of senior military and political leaders, in the heyday of the Cold War, which argued for preventive attacks against the Soviet Union in the 1950s and the destruction of Chinese nuclear facilities in the 1960s. Advocates of these defence strategies viewed Stalin and Mao much like Saddam Hussein was viewed in the mobilization to war – as 'wildly aggressive fanatics' who were irrational and not subject to the normal constraints of deterrence strategies.[46] But, more than anything else, as an exercise in prevention, the war in Iraq can best be understood within the grand design of balance of power politics. At a stroke, it recast the Middle East to advance American material and geopolitical interests and signalled in the strongest possible terms the arrival of the new doctrine, namely that no country or alliance dare challenge the overwhelming superiority of American force.

Looked at dispassionately, with no concern for morality, it is possible to see how a cold logic of national interest drove Bush's prevention doctrine. But we see no possible case for Blair's complicity in the implementation of that doctrine: hence Principle 8.

Principle 8   Pre-emptive war is justified but preventive war is morally and strategically wrong

The repeated application of the concept of pre-emptive war to the war in Iraq glosses the critical distinction between necessary and appropriate self-defensive (pre-emption) and an optional, unwarranted, offensive attack (prevention) to secure a favourable balance of power in the absence of 'just fear'. A comparison of the American National Security Strategy and the British post-9/11 New Chapter of its Strategic Defence Review, produced a scant two months apart, underscores very significant differences in doctrine and perspective between the two countries. The USA asserts the right to prevent any challenge to its overwhelming superiority; the UK, in contrast, focuses on defence diplomacy and conflict prevention. This gap in strategic visions, as well as America's unbridled imperial arrogance, should have been viewed as a 'red-line' (see Principle 1), providing a firm basis for the UK to withdraw unconditional support from the American position and resist echoing Bush's unethical, unwise and intentionally misleading claim that the invasion of Iraq could be justified as a pre-emptive war.

An Alternative Foreign Policy

This is a daunting age in which to conduct an effective, ethically sound and progressive foreign policy. It is one plagued by endemic human rights abuses that warrant intervention, and by horrific security threats that require concerted responses on many fronts, including the use of force. International law as well as the institutions for global governance can be no more effective than the most powerful states will allow; and this is a particularly grave problem when, as now, the leading hegemonic power exhibits little interest in truly collective or multilateral measures. And the UK must operate in this context constrained both by resource limits and by a diminished capacity to fundamentally change the course set by the United States. So the challenges are profound; but this does not mean that a Labour Government should allow itself to be trapped by unconditional support for the USA, or to shrink from its responsibilities to conduct an ethical foreign policy. On the contrary, the aftermath of the invasion of Iraq is precisely the time when that Government should consider the adoption of an alternative foreign policy: one grounded in the historic mission of the Labour Party, mindful of the ethical lessons that can be drawn from the war in Iraq and cognizant of the dangers of unchecked American arrogance.

The eight principles we have introduced constitute key elements of a coherent, sensible, alternative framework for contemporary British foreign policy – one that would revitalize a progressive Labour Party vision, bring together foreign and domestic affairs, and put Britain in a position to advance legitimate national interests. In introducing our alternative, we will integrate these ethical principles with the best elements of the Old Labour and New Labour traditions discussed in chapter 6, brought up to date and adjusted as they must be to meet the challenges of the post-9/11 world.

Our alternative is shaped in very important ways by the socialist foreign policy critique laid out in chapter 6, drawing in particular on its emphasis on internationalism, its rejection of militarism and its powerfully articulated commitment to the ethical conduct of foreign affairs. Like the socialist foreign policy critics of British imperialism, we reject any use of British foreign policy to secure commercial or financial advantage. For this reason, we require that the aims justifying the use of force in intervention must exclusively be humanitarian (see Principle 6). At the same time, we part company with the strongly pacifist strands of the socialist foreign policy tradition. As Kosovo, Rwanda, Liberia and many other tragic cases of the systematic and catastrophic abuse of human rights for political ends make clear, our era cannot ethically condone unqualified pacifism. Principle 7 articulates a positive responsibility to intervene with force to prevent or contain humanitarian catastrophe. And of course, the terror attacks of 11 September provide a wholly legitimate basis for a coordinated campaign that includes limited, authorized use of force from a multilateral platform, as part of an integrated strategy to disrupt and disable terror groups (Principle 3). We recognize, however, that the effect of force is limited and ephemeral – in this imperfect and dangerous world, we can do no better than manage the risks of terror and weapons of mass destruction effectively enough to reduce their strategic effect and limit the risks to acceptable levels (Principle 2).

The alternative we propose takes little from Labour's traditional foreign policy, beyond conceding a pragmatic view that the defence of state and nation are the necessary attributes of any party of government. It rejects Tony Blair's defiant internationalism as a monumental strategic blunder that betrayed the good intentions of the 'force for good' aspirations of New Labour's post-1997 foreign policy vision, and that drew instead on the worst Atlanticist and imperialist elements of Labour's traditional foreign policy heritage. Rather, we are convinced that an ethical foreign policy for the UK can best emerge from a synthesis of the socialist foreign policy critique and a critical engagement with New Labour's offensive multilateralism. That synthesis is all the easier because of the degree to which New Labour's post-1997 foreign policy approach already displayed important continuities with the socialist critics of Old Labour: through

its resolute commitment to internationalism, its call for more effective multilateral institutions and its commitment to debt reduction as
part of a broader project to advance international community and
address the challenges of global interdependence. These were and
remain laudable goals; but New Labour's reading of globalization
bears an unfortunate kinship with the uncritical association of national
interest and global commercial interests that was a core element of
the traditional foreign policy framework – and this limits the extent
to which the UK can be a force for good in global economic affairs.
It is clear that for both Tony Blair and Gordon Brown globalization
has hastened the emergence of a global economic system beyond the
control of any given state: one in which competitiveness, comparative advantage and growth require strict adherence to the credos of
fiscal and monetary stability. Hence, New Labour economic policy
orientations, goals and instruments are focused acutely on global
competitiveness within a neo-liberal mindset, accepting the logic of
winners and losers and doing nothing substantial to abate the alarming development gap between North and South. In any resetting of
New Labour's foreign policy, this neo-liberal mindset will also have
to go.

   With regard to security and humanitarian intervention, New Labour's foreign policy before 9/11 focused on the lessons of Kosovo,
connected security issues to global interdependence and called for
reforms of the Security Council. The British role in enforcement
actions in Sierra Leone in 2000 confirmed the UK's willingness to
assume the responsibility to intervene militarily for humanitarian
reasons in a manner consistent with Principles 6 and 7 as laid out
here. Any New Labour government that placed at front and centre
its commitment to Security Council reform and the comprehensive
enhancement of multilateral institutions would almost certainly welcome with open arms our proposals for enhancing the authority of
the Security Council in authorizing the use of force (Principle 4) and
for the quick transfer of post-intervention powers to a multilateral
authority at the lowest possible effective level (Principle 5). All of
which makes Tony Blair's rush to war in lock-step with the Bush
Administration not just misguided, but also in tension with the more
progressive elements of New Labour thinking on foreign policy. And
to think that that rush could have been prevented if Blair had sub-
mitted the Anglo-American coalition to the kinds of reasonable conditions and 'red-lines' so tantalizingly proposed by his own Chief of
Defence Staff, Michael Boyce (Principle 1)!

   The ethical principles we have drawn from our critical reassess-
ment of the key security, humanitarian and governance challenges of

the post-9/11 world fit well with the most cosmopolitan, forward-looking moments in the Labour Party's foreign policy heritage. Taken together, these principles crystallize an alternative approach to foreign policy that offers a clear path forward and demonstrates that ethical values and effective policy must be applied in tandem to achieve maximum effect.

An ethical foreign policy alternative

Promote a foreign policy that affirms internationalism and multilateralism as ethical aims as well as practical goals to maximize UK policy as a force for good and to respond to the security threats of the post-9/11 world. Recognize that security against terrorist attacks requires a coordinated campaign integrating the authorized use of force with ideological, political, diplomatic and judicial initiatives, and accept that force is limited in effect. Attention to the causes of terror – as well as historic Labour Party concerns for social justice – mandate a new determination to reduce the North/South development gap. Effective foreign policy requires the reform and empowerment of global institutions and a rigorous application of standards and benchmarks defining the rightful grounds for humanitarian intervention, affirming humanitarian responsibilities that are distinct from economic and geopolitical advantage, and facilitating the complex cultural negotiations that make or break intervention in multi-ethnic societies. The UK should consider all coalitions conditional and refuse to cross 'red-lines' that compromise core values and ethical principles.

We are convinced that the ethical lapses of judgement at the heart of Britain's participation in the war in Iraq are sufficiently grave and pervasive that, even if the empirical claims by Bush and Blair about Iraqi threats had been accurate, the war in Iraq would still have been tragically wrong on ethical grounds alone. For once the rules of the game that constitute the international order have been (as here) ignored with impunity – or rewritten in a dismissive and pre-emptory manner by the dominant power in the system and its ally – the door to chaos in international affairs is inevitably opened. In both moral and practical terms, it matters when great states rewrite the rules to justify war, by extending self-defence from pre-emptive action against imminent attack to the far more controversial realm of preventive action against potential attack over the horizon. It matters when powerful states elect to use force in the name of a very limited 'coalition of the willing' without the authorization of the United Nations and in the teeth of massive popular opposition. For then new rules are seen to apply; which is why, in this case, the repercussions of the preventive use of force, hegemonic bullying and the use and abuse of the United Nations are so profoundly worrying. Tony Blair's decision to sign up to the blatantly self-serving doctrine of a right-wing American defence establishment hell-bent on war is all the more confounding because far better alternatives were readily available in the foreign policy legacies of his own party. In our view, Tony Blair's policies on Iraq compromised the nation, sacrificed the party and facilitated a brutal war that cannot be justified on ethical grounds; and because they did, now is overwhelmingly the time to replace those policies with others. The bushwhacking of New Labour has gone on long enough.

Notes

Studies of this kind are only possible because of the quantity and range of internet sites that carry the full text of public statements made by the key figures in the policy-making process. Among these are the official websites of the White House, the Pentagon, the State Department, 10 Downing Street, the Foreign and Commonwealth Office, Select Committees of the House of Commons and the Hutton Inquiry. Important material is available too on the internet sites of major news outlets. So unless indicated otherwise, the speeches quoted in this text have been drawn from the following internet sites:

www.whitehouse/news/releases
www.whitehouse/gov/infocus/iraq/iraqarchive
www.whitehouse/vicepres
www.defencelink.mil/speeches
www.state.gov/secretary/rm
www.number-10.gov.uk
www.parliament.the-station . . . select/cm/liaisn
www.parliament.the-station . . . select/cmfaff
www.guardian.co.uk/Iraq/story
www.news.bbc.co.uk

For ease of access to these footnotes, we have decided not to record here the full website reference for each speech; but that information is available from the authors if required.

CHAPTER 1   THE PROBLEM OF BLAIR'S WAR

1   See, for example, 'Hinesville is the armpit of the world. Right now I'll take the armpit', *Guardian*, 16 July 2003, p. 3.

2   These were the famous sixteen words inserted into the 2003 State of the Union Address. By July the CIA had admitted its error, and Condoleezza Rice's deputy (Stephen Hadley) had conceded that the claim had slipped into the Address by accident and on his watch, and had offered to resign. The sixteen words were: 'The British Government has learned that Saddam Hussein recently sought significant quantities of uranium from Africa.' Unfortunately for the claim, however, Saddam Hussein had not, and the White House had been told that he had not! (On this, see 'A question of trust', *Time Magazine*, 21 July 2003, pp. 22–6.) The matter became even more significant in late September 2003, when the man who told the White House that the claim was false, Joseph Wilson, accused the Administration of leaking to the press the information that his wife was an undercover CIA agent, working on weapons of mass destruction.

3   Jack Straw, in evidence to the Foreign Affairs Select Committee, 24 June 2003.

4   The Interim Report was generally written up in the press as a confirmation of 'what many had come to suspect in the months since Baghdad fell. In sum, Saddam Hussein's regime did not possess useable biological, chemical or nuclear weapons when the war was launched' (*Guardian*, Friday 3 October 2003). In fact, the report was more cautious than that. David Kay told Congress only that 'we have not yet found stocks of weapons, but we are not yet at the point where we can definitively say either that such weapon stocks do not exist or that they existed before the war'.

5   *Guardian*, 19 August 2003 and 23 September 2003, reporting ICM poll results.

6   *Financial Times*, 10 September 2003, p. 2; and BBC News, 4 August 2003.

7   Cited in the *Independent*, 16 July 2003, p. 1.

8   Senator Graham, reported in the *Financial Times*, 28 July 2003, p. 1.

9   *Guardian*, polling 108 out of the 409 Labour MPs, 27 September 2003.

10   When asked if it was 'now time for Tony Blair to resign and hand over to someone else', 50 per cent of those polled said they agreed, 39 per cent said they disagreed and 11 per cent said they did not know.

11   The Prime Minister's Speech to Congress, 18 July 2003.

CHAPTER 2   NEW LABOUR: A LEADING FORCE FOR GOOD IN THE WORLD?

1   The Prime Minister's Speech to Congress, 18 July 2003.

2   *Hansard*, 15 February 1996, col. 1146. For a full briefing, see M. Pythian, *Arming Iraq* (Boston, MA: North Eastern University Press, 1997).

3   *Hansard*, 15 February 1996, cols 1145–6.

4   Labour Party, 1997 General Election Manifesto, *New Labour, Because Britain Deserves Better*, pp. 37–9.

5 Robin Cook, 'Britain's new approach to the world', speech to the 1997 Labour Party annual conference, *LPACR*, 1997, p. 132.

6 Tony Blair, 'Doctrine of the international community', speech to the Economic Club of Chicago, Hilton Hotel, Chicago, 22 April 1999. The speech is available at <http://www.globalpolicy.org/globaliz/politics/blair.htm>

7 Robin Cook, 'Britain's future in Europe', speech at Britain in Europe campaign event, 23 November 1999.

8 Tony Blair, 'Britain's role in the EU and the Transatlantic Alliance', speech to the Associated Press, London, 15 December 1998.

9 Tony Blair, 'Committed to Europe, reforming Europe', Ghent speech, 23 February 2000.

10 Robin Cook, 'Britain's future in Europe'.

11 Labour Party, 2001 General Election Manifesto, *Ambitions for Britain*, p. 38.

12 See Tony Blair's speech to the 2001 Labour Party annual conference, *LPACR*, 2001, p. 93.

13 On this, see R. Ramesh (ed.), *The War We Could Not Stop* (London: Guardian, 2003), p. 14.

14 Cited in N. M. Ahmed, *Behind the War on Terror* (East Sussex: Clairview, 2003), p. 191.

15 Speech by the Prime Minister, at his arrival ceremony at the White House, 5 February 1998.

16 M. Wickham-Jones, 'Labour's trajectory in foreign affairs: the moral crusade of a pivotal power?', in R. Little and M. Wickham-Jones (eds), *New Labour's Foreign Policy* (Manchester: Manchester University Press, 2000), p. 24.

17 The Prime Minister's statement in Parliament concerning Iraq, 17 December 1998.

18 Interview on NBC's *Meet the Press*, 2 January 2000.

19 Oral evidence to the Foreign Affairs Committee, 24 June 2003.

20 Tony Blair, 'A new era of international partnership', speech to the United Nations General Assembly, New York, 21 September 1998.

21 Robin Cook, 'Mission statement for the Foreign and Commonwealth Office', May 1997.

22 Ibid.

23 R. Little, 'Conclusions: the ethics and the strategy of Labour's Third Way in foreign policy', in Little and Wickham-Jones, *New Labour's Foreign Policy*, p. 261.

24 On this, see M. Pythian, *The Politics of British Arms Sales since 1964* (Manchester: Manchester University Press), pp. 287–308; and N. Cooper, 'The pariah agenda and New Labour's ethical foreign policy', in Little and Wickham-Jones, *New Labour's Foreign Policy*, pp. 147–67. Cooper's overall assessment is damning. 'Judged solely on its own language,' he wrote, 'Labour's arms sales policy is less ethical than its own policy in the 1980s, less ethical than that of a number of other states, less ethical than the EU code, and little different from the ethically challenged approach of its Conservative predecessors' (p. 163).

25 *Hansard*, Legg Inquiry, 27 July 1998, col. 19.
26 Robin Cook, speech to the 1995 Labour Party annual conference, *LPACR*, 1995, p. 190.
27 Will Bartlett, 'Simply the right thing to do: Labour goes to war', in Little and Wickham-Jones, *New Labour's Foreign Policy*, p. 133.
28 Ibid., pp. 133–4.
29 Robin Cook, cited in John Lloyd, 'Cook declares total war on fascism', *New Statesman*, 3 May 1999, p. 8.

CHAPTER 3   THE AMERICAN CALL TO ARMS

1   Presidential radio address, 15 September 2001.
2   Presidential address to Congress, 20 September 2001.
3   Colin Powell, remarks to the press, 14 September 2001.
4   Donald Rumsfeld, 'A new kind of war', *New York Times*, 27 September 2001; and address at Whiteman Air Force Base, 19 October 2001.
5   Paul Wolfowitz, speech to the American Jewish Congress, 22 October 2001.
6   Paul Wolfowitz, speaking on Iraq to the International Institute for Strategic Studies, London, 2 December 2002.
7   We are sure that it is, since Woodward was the *Washington Post* reporter who (with Carl Bernstein) broke the Watergate story and has cultivated privileged access to Washington insiders for decades, seldom to better effect than at present.
8   Bob Woodward, *Bush At War* (New York: Simon and Schuster, 2002), pp. 49, 60.
9   Ibid., p. 61.
10 Colin Powell, remarks to the press, 14 September 2001.
11 Ibid., 13 September 2001.
12 Ibid., 14 October 2001.
13 Ibid., 5 December 2001.
14 Paul Wolfowitz, in a prepared statement for the House and Senate Armed Services Committees, 3 and 4 October 2001.
15 Donald Rumsfeld, statement to the NATO Council, Brussels, Belgium, 18 December 2001.
16 George W. Bush, State of the Union Address to Congress, 29 January 2002. Technically, the claim that Iraq had kicked out the inspectors was incorrect. As was mentioned in chapter 2, they were withdrawn (in December 1988).
17 Ibid., p. 2 (emphasis added).
18 S. Fidler, 'Just when did the President decide to go to war?' *Financial Times*, 27 March 2003, p. 5.
19 Press Conference: Prime Minister Tony Blair and President George Bush, 6 April 2002.
20 Remarks by the President, Ridgewood Golf Club, Waco, Texas, 10 August 2002.

21 *The National Security Strategy of the United States*, September 2002, pp. 14, v, 15 (emphases added).
22 Remarks by the President at the 2002 Graduation Exercise of the United States Military Academy West Point, New York, 1 June 2002.
23 Woodward, *Bush At War*, pp. 332–4.
24 Ibid., pp. 332–6.
25 Vice-President Cheney, address to the Veterans of Foreign Wars National Convention, 27 August 2002.
26 Woodward, *Bush At War*, pp. 345–6.
27 Colin Powell, remarks to the press, 4 September 2002.
28 Ibid.
29 The secondary commentaries already available to us seem in agreement that 'as Bush delivered his speech, the vital reference to adopting the UN route dropped off his teleprompter, apparently because of a technical problem' (R. Ramesh (ed.), *The War We Could Not Stop* (London: Guardian, 2003), p. 26; also Woodward, *Bush At War*, p. 348). They agree too that the President saved the day by ad-libbing the lines in, remembering their presence in what Woodward called 'draft 24' of the speech. What the secondary commentaries do not agree upon, however, is whether that draft had talked of 'resolution*s*' (the Woodward account) or only of 'the need for a new UN resolutio*n*' (Ramesh). According to Ramesh, at least, the Bush ad-libbing of a US commitment to the pursuit of new resolution*s* in the 'plural was to have big consequences for the diplomatic campaign' that then ensued.
30 Donald Rumsfeld, testifying before the House Armed Services Committee, 18 September 2002.
31 Ibid.
32 Ibid.
33 President Bush, addressing the nation from Cincinnati, Ohio, 7 October 2002.
34 Paul Wolfowitz, speaking on Iraq to the Fletcher Conference, Washington, DC, 16 October 2002.
35 Paul Wolfowitz, speaking on Iraq to the Defense Forum Foundation, Washington, DC, 18 October 2002.
36 Paul Wolfowitz, speaking to the Council on Foreign Relations, New York, 23 January 2003.
37 Paul Wolfowitz, speaking to the World Affairs Council and the Commonwealth Club, San Francisco, 6 December 2002.
38 'Powell briefing: key points', Wednesday 5 February 2003.
39 George W. Bush, State of the Union Address, 28 January 2003.
40 Colin Powell, remarks to the press, 5 December 2002.
41 Ibid., 27 January 2003.
42 Paul Wolfowitz, speaking to the Council on Foreign Relations, New York, 23 January 2003.
43 Colin Powell, remarks to the press, 5 December 2002.
44 Ibid., 27 January 2003.

45 Press conference: Prime Minister Tony Blair and President Bush at the White House, 31 January 2003.
46 As we will see later, this was the dossier that was later much criticized for being in part plagiarized from an unpublished PhD thesis written more than a decade earlier and/or from an academic article by the same author, to which no attribution was made.
47 Powell briefing: key points', Wednesday 5 February 2003.
48 For an authoritative account of this period, see paragraphs 11–77 of the House of Commons Foreign Affairs Committee, 10th report of session 2002–3, *Foreign Policy Aspects of the War Against Terrorism*, HC 405, London, The Stationery Office Limited, 31 July 2003.
49 Colin Powell, remarks to the press, 27 January 2003.
50 President George Bush, addressing the nation from the White House, 18 March 2003.
51 Ibid.

CHAPTER 4   ANSWERING THE CALL

1   Prime Minister's briefing to the press, 21 September 2001.
2   Prime Minister's statement to the House of Commons, 8 October 2001.
3   Ibid.
4   Prime Ministerial statement in response to terrorist attacks in the United States, 11 September 2001.
5   Edited transcript of an interview given by the Prime Minister to Larry King, CNN, 6 November 2001.
6   Prime Minister's briefing to the press, 21 September 2001.
7   Transcript of a press conference with Prime Minister Tony Blair and US Secretary of State Colin Powell, 11 December 2001.
8   Prime Minister's interview with CNN, 16 September 2001.
9   Transcript of the press conference between Prime Minister Tony Blair and President Bush, 8 November 2001.
10 Prime Minister's statement to the House of Commons, 8 October 2001.
11 Edited transcript of an interview given by the Prime Minister to Larry King, CNN, 6 November 2001.
12 Prime Minister's interview with CNN, 16 September 2001.
13 Press conference given by Prime Minister Tony Blair to Arab journalists, 19 October 2001.
14 Ibid.
15 Prime Minister's interview with CNN, 16 September 2001.
16 Press conference given by Prime Minister Tony Blair to Arab journalists, 19 October 2001.
17 Transcript of the Prime Minister's statement on Afghanistan, 13 November 2001.
18 Prime Minister's interview with CNN, 16 September 2001.
19 Prime Minister's briefing to the press, 21 September 2001.

20   Press conference given by Prime Minister Tony Blair to Arab journalists, 19 October 2001.
21   Prime Minister's briefing to the press, 21 September 2001.
22   Press conference given by Prime Minister Tony Blair to Arab journalists, 19 October 2001.
23   Press conference with Prime Minister Tony Blair and US Secretary of State Colin Powell, 11 December 2001.
24   Jack Straw, 'Re-ordering the world', speech to the Foreign Policy Centre, London, 25 March 2002.
25   Jack Straw, 'Principles of a modern global community', speech at the Mansion House, London, 10 April 2002.
26   Press conference: Prime Minister Tony Blair and President George Bush, 6 April 2002.
27   The full text is available at <http://www.pm.gov.uk/output/Page1712.asp>
28   *Guardian*, 15 January 2003, p. 5.
29   'Less discreet British officials point to string of diplomatic tussles in which they say Mr Blair and the cause of caution came out the victors. The key moment came on a beautiful September day in Maryland last year, when . . . despite hostile questioning by the hawkish Mr Cheney, Mr Blair capped months of steady British pressure and secured an agreement from the President to pursue the campaign against President Hussein through the UN' (ibid., p. 6). Tony Blair rather confirmed this himself later, when rebutting Clare Short's claim that it was in September that he (and George Bush) decided to go to war. He told the Liaison Committee this: 'I cannot actually remember her being at Camp David but . . . let me say to you not merely is that untrue; it is the opposite of the truth. I will tell you exactly what I agreed with George Bush back at Camp David: that we should proceed through the United Nations because that was the proper thing to do, that the best way of avoiding war was to get UN weapons inspectors back in there with a clear undertaking from the international community, that if they were not able to do their job properly, if there was not the fullest co-operation, then there would be military action that would follow' (Minutes of Evidence, Liaison Committee, 28 July 2003).
30   An unnamed 'New Labour heavyweight', cited in the *Guardian*, 15 January 2003, p. 4.
31   Prime Minister's address to British ambassadors in London, 7 January 2003.
32   Remarks by the President and Prime Minister in photo opportunity, Camp David, Maryland, 7 September 2002.
33   Jack Straw, 'Failed and failing states', speech to the European Research Institute, Birmingham, 6 September 2002.
34   Jack Straw, 'The UK and the US: a partnership for stability and prosperity', speech to the Chicago Council for Foreign Relations, 15 October 2002.
35   Tony Blair's address to the TUC, 10 September 2002.
36   Ibid.

37 It was this claim in particular that – according to the BBC later – was *added* to the dossier on the orders of Downing Street, to make the whole thing 'sexier'. It was added, according to the intelligence sources used by the BBC, 'against our wishes because it wasn't reliable' (BBC, 29 May 2003). It was this claim that sparked the great row between the BBC and the Government, and produced both the Foreign Affairs Committee report, *The Decision to go to War in Iraq* (The Stationery Office Ltd, 7 July 2003) and the Hutton Inquiry. The Committee report exonerated the Prime Minister's official spokesman of any doctoring of the report, but criticized the emphasis placed by the Government on this 45-minute claim when introducing it. 'The 45 minute claim', it said, 'did not warrant the prominence given to it in the dossier' (paragraph 70 of the report). Hans Blix, the UN's chief weapons inspector, later criticized the claim too, calling it 'pretty far off the mark' (BBC News, 13 July 2003). Evidence to the later Hutton Inquiry also made it clear that, even if Alastair Campbell hadn't put pressure on those drafting the September dossier, others in the Prime Minister's immediate circle had sent emails suggesting that paragraphs be redrafted. That redrafting was designed to avoid creating the impression that Saddam Hussein would only use chemical and biological weapons against western troops if he were attacked by them. However, the Hutton Inquiry eventually if controversially cleared the Government of any duplicity in relation to both the September dossier and the subsequent naming of the BBC's source.

38 *Iraq's Weapons of Mass Destruction: The Assessment of the British Government*, September 2002, p. 6. This was the so-called 'Niger' claim that made its way into the 2003 State of the Union Address, but which was found subsequently to be entirely false.

39 Foreword by Tony Blair to the 24 September dossier, p. 3.

40 Prime Minister's Iraq statement to Parliament, 24 September 2002.

41 Prime Minister's address at the Lord Mayor's banquet, 11 November 2002.

42 Tony Blair's statement in response to the passing of UN Security Council Resolution 1441, 8 November 2002.

43 Ibid. (our emphasis). It is noticeable just how different the Blair position was prior to the war from that of the Bush Administration, a dilemma from which Blair was eventually only extricated by the intransigence of Saddam Hussein. Questioned on the dilemma in April 2003, he said this: '[T]he logic of that position has been somewhat uncomfortable, frankly for me and for others, that if Saddam had voluntarily disarmed he could have remained in place. Now personally I think his regime would have changed its very nature through that process, but on the other hand he would have remained in power. In one sense I feel more comfortable with the position now where we are saying quite plainly to people the only way now to disarm him is to remove the regime' (press conference, 8 April 2003).

44 Alastair Campbell told the Liaison Committee that Tony Blair in those months worked 'round the clock, flat out, trying to keep this thing on

the United Nations' route as a means of avoiding conflict' (oral evidence to the Liaison Committee, 30 June 2003).

45   The process by which the February dossier had been compiled was also heavily criticized in the Foreign Affairs Committee's 9th report, *The Decision to go to War in Iraq*. See, in particular, paragraphs 108–39.

46   'Blair defends al-Qaeda claim', BBC News, 5 February 2003.

47   Press conference: Prime Minister Tony Blair and President Bush at the White House, 31 January 2003.

48   Prime Minister's address at the Lord Mayor's banquet, 11 November 2002 (emphasis added).

49   Address to the International Institute for Strategic Studies, 11 February 2003.

50   The global figures for anti-war protesters that weekend was possibly 30 million, with at least 6 million in Europe (*Guardian*, 17 February 2003, p. 6).

51   Tony Blair, 'The price of my conviction', *Observer*, 16 February 2003, p. 20 (emphasis added).

52   In mid-February 2003, 52 per cent of those polled opposed going to war. By mid-April, it should be noted, as Baghdad fell, that percentage fell to 23 per cent (*Guardian*, 15 April 2003, p. 1). That marked the peak of Blair's gaining of a 'Basra factor'.

53   *Hansard*, 17 March 2003, cols. 726–8.

54   John Kampfner reports that Jack Straw made a last-minute plea to Tony Blair to offer moral support to the USA but no immediate military support (John Kampfner, *Blair's War* (London: The Free Press, 2003), p. 303).

55   *Guardian*, 19 March 2003, p. 1.

56   Prime Minister's address to the nation, 21 March 2003.

CHAPTER 5   THE JUSTIFICATIONS FOR WAR

1   The initial 'coalition of the willing' comprised the USA, the UK, Australia, Bahrain, Bulgaria, Croatia, the Czech Republic, Hungary, Italy, Jordan, Kuwait, Oman, Portugal, Qatar, Romania, Saudi Arabia, Slovakia, Spain, Turkey, the UAE and Ukraine. Only the UK and Australia actually committed troops (45,000 and 2,000 respectively).

2   Prime Minister's statement to Parliament on the NATO summit, 25 November 2002.

3   'In Washington on September 26, Secretary of Defense Donald Rumsfeld claimed he had "bulletproof" evidence of ties between Saddam and al-Qaeda' (S. Ackerman and J. B. Judis, 'The first casualty', *The New Republic*, 30 June 2003, p. 14). So too did CIA Director George Tennet in his 7 October 2002 open letter to the chairman of the Senate Intelligence Committee, Senator Graham, in which he wrote: 'We have solid reporting of senior level contacts between Iraq and al-Qaeda going back a decade, credible information indicates that Iraq and al-Qaeda have

discussed safe haven and reciprocal non-aggression; since Operation Enduring Freedom we have solid evidence of the presence in Iraq of al-Qaeda members, including some that have been in Baghdad; we have credible reporting that al-Qaeda leaders sought contacts in Iraq who could help them acquire WMD [weapons of mass destruction] capabilities; and the reporting also stated that Iraq has provided training to al-Qaeda members in the areas of poisons and gases and making conventional bombs.' This might usefully be contrasted with Rumsfeld's later agnosticism when asked about a poll indicating that nearly 70 per cent of the US population believed that Saddam Hussein was personally involved in the events of 9/11. 'I've not seen any indication that would lead me to believe that I could say that' was his non-denial denial (*Associated Press*, 17 September 2003).

4 President Bush announcing that major combat operations in Iraq have ended, 1 May 2003, at sea off the coast of San Diego, California.

5 President Bush, addressing the American Enterprise Institute, 27 February 2003.

6 Paul Wolfowitz, speaking on Iraq to the International Institute for Strategic Studies, London, 2 December 2002.

7 Jack Straw, addressing the International Institute for Strategic Studies, 11 February 2003.

8 President Bush, addressing the American Enterprise Institute, 27 February 2003.

9 *Financial Times*, 11 September 2003, p. 6.

10 Address to the International Institute for Strategic Studies, 11 February 2003.

11 Quoted in the *Guardian*, 26 February 2003.

12 Address to the International Institute for Strategic Studies, 11 February 2003.

13 The Prime Minister interviewed on the future of Iraq, 4 April 2003.

14 Prime Minister's statement to Parliament on the NATO summit, 25 November 2002.

15 As he told the House of Commons on 18 March 2003, 'I have never put the justification for action as regime change'.

16 Victoria Clarke, Pentagon, 1 April 2003 (BBC News, 1 April 2003).

17 It should be noted, however, that, when releasing the review of human rights, the State Department spokesperson said this in response to a BBC question on whether Iraq was the world's worst violator of human rights: 'No, I would think that that honor goes to North Korea.' The Pentagon was quick to dispute that ranking; but what they could not dispute was the presence, in the list of systematic violators of human rights, of 14 of the 49 countries then listed by the USA as among 'the coalition of the willing' (BBC, 1 April 2003).

18 This was definitely the view of the UK Select Committee on Foreign Affairs which, in its tenth report of session 2002–3, *Foreign Policy Aspects of the War Against Terrorism*, published 30 July 2003, observed that 'in the short term, al-Qaeda's stance on Iraq may encourage

some misguided individuals or small groups to try to commit terrorist acts, including against coalition forces in Iraq, and elsewhere in the region or further away' (paragraph 176). It was also the view of senior British intelligence chiefs, given to Tony Blair in February 2003 (and therefore *before* the invasion), that 'the likelihood of weapons of mass destruction falling into the hands of al-Qaeda or other terrorist groups would be increased by the collapse of Saddam Hussein's regime' (*Financial Times*, 12 September 2003, p. 1). 'Al-Qaeda and associated interests', Blair was warned by Whitehall's joint intelligence committee, 'continue to represent by far the greatest threat to western interests, and that threat would be heightened by military action against Iraq' (*Guardian*, 12 September 2003, p. 1).

19   When challenged on this by the Foreign Affairs Committee in September 2002, the UK Foreign Secretary said this: 'No one has ever suggested that Saddam Hussein is directly behind the al-Qaeda organization, and I have never seen that suggested. Now others may have seen that suggested, but I have not. I would then go on to say that given the fact that Saddam Hussein's regime has unquestionably been supportive of terrorist organizations in the Middle East, and given his hatred for the United States, which is visceral, it is reasonable to see that he has some sympathy with the al-Qaeda regime, and therefore for us to look for evidence . . . nothing at least that we have seen so far suggests that Iraq was involved in the September attacks' (oral evidence, 25 September 2002).

20   For calm and expert testimony to this effect, see paragraph 178 of the Foreign Affairs Committee's *Foreign Policy Aspects of the War Against Terrorism*. Writing just before the invasion, the former weapons inspector Scott Ritter put it more bluntly: 'This one is patently absurd. Saddam is a secular dictator. He has spent the last 30 years declaring war against Islamic fundamentalism, crushing it. He fought a war against Iran in part because of Islamic fundamentalism. The Iraqis have laws on the books today that provide for an immediate death sentence for proselytizing in the name of Wahabism, or indeed any Islam, but they are particularly virulent in their hatred of Wahabs, which is of course Osama bin Laden's religion. Osama bin Laden has a history of hating Saddam Hussein. He's called him an apostate, somebody who needs to be killed' (S. Ritter and W. Rivers Pitt, *War On Iraq* (London: Profile Books, 2002), p. 45).

21   There was much speculation in the US press in the summer of 2003 that this was why President Bush declined to declassify the section of the report of the congressional inquiry into the 11 September attacks that dealt with the Saudis, that, as one of the Senators who saw it commented, the report contained 'compelling evidence that a foreign government provided direct support through officials and agents of that government to some of the September 11 hijackers' (Senator Graham, quoted in the *New York Times*, 30 July 2003).

22   It was even less clear that the Iraqi regime posed such a danger to the UK. As the former Tory Minister Kenneth Clarke put it in the first

House of Commons debate on the invasion: 'I don't believe there is any evidence of links to al-Qaeda. I don't believe the [Iraqis] pose a threat to New York or London. I think that's an insult to our intelligence' (*Guardian*, 2 February 2003, p. 5).

23   One of the most bizarre aspects of this whole story is the manner in which the Bush Administration chose to treat North Korea, Iran and Iraq so differently: choosing to invade the country that had only the potential of such weapons while choosing the diplomatic route against the countries that had them already (and in North Korea's case were publicly proclaiming their possession of enough plutonium to make six atomic bombs).

24   David Usborne, 'WMD just a convenient excuse for war, admits Wolfowitz', *Independent*, 30 May 2003.

25   Cited in ibid.

26   N. Kristof, 'Save our Spooks', *New York Times*, 30 May 2003.

27   This was suggested by Donald Rumsfeld himself, late in May 2003, when he told the Council of Foreign Relations in New York: 'we don't know what happened. It is also possible that [Saddam's government] decided they would destroy them prior to a conflict' (quoted in the *Independent*, 29 May 2003).

28   Polly Toynbee, 'Did Blair lie to us?', *Guardian*, 30 May 2003.

29   *New York Times*, 4 May 2003.

30   Ibid.

31   Quoted in the *Guardian*, 30 May 2003.

32   Robin Cook made this point in his 'Britain must not be suckered a second time', *Independent*, 30 May 2003.

33   It should also be noted in this regard that Reagan's Assistant Secretary of State Elliott Abrams was selected by George W. Bush as the National Security Council's senior director for democracy, human rights and international operations. Abrams pleaded guilty to two misdemeanor counts of lying to Congress during the Iran Contra hearings and was subsequently pardoned by George Bush, Sr.

34   It is worth noting that Falluja 2, the chemical plant identified by Colin Powell in his address to the UN, was actually built with the secret backing of the Thatcher Government, and was built – by a UK subsidiary of a German company – even though at the time (1985) 'senior officials recorded in writing that Saddam Hussein was actively gassing his opponents and that there was a strong possibility that the . . . plant was intended by the Iraqis to make mustard gas', *Guardian*, 6 March 2003, p. 1.

35   *Guardian*, 18 February 2003, p. 19.

36   Ritter and Rivers Pitt, *War on Iraq*, p. 5. For a similar argument, heavily supported by a survey of available evidence, see M. Pythian, *Arming Iraq* (Boston, MA: North Eastern University Press, 1997), p. 309.

37   On this, see J. Simpson, 'A dictator of mass destruction', in BBC News, *The Battle for Baghdad* (London: BBC, 2003), p. 141. There was a fascinating exchange about that visit between Secretary of Defense

Rumsfeld and Senator Robert Byrd prior to the invasion. Appearing before a Senate committee, Rumsfeld was pressed by Byrd on the veracity of a *Newsweek* article documenting the secret arming of Saddam Hussein in 1982 by the Reagan Administration – armaments that included tanks, computers and video cameras for political surveillance, helicopters and, 'most unsettling' to the Senator, 'numerous shipments of bacteria/fungi/ protozoa' to the Iraqi Atomic Energy Commission. Noting that the Reagan Administration first denied, and then conceded, that it knew that the Iraqis had used chemical weapons against the Iranians, and that Rumsfeld himself had – at Reagan's behest – travelled to Baghdad immediately after the event, Byrd asked him: 'Now, can this possibly be true . . . Are we in fact now facing the possibility of reaping what we have sown?' The Secretary of Defense would not be drawn. 'I doubt it', he said, and in any event, 'I was not in government at that time, except as a special envoy for a period of months. So one ought not to rely on me as the best source as to what happened in that mid-80s period that you were describing' (testimony before the Senate Armed Services Committee, 19 September 2002). A classic case of a non-denial denial?

38 Robin Cook, 'Why I had to leave the Cabinet', *Guardian*, 18 March 2003, p. 26.
39 This was certainly the view of Senator Robert Byrd of West Virginia, one of the few Democratic senators prepared to offer sustained and principled resistance to the Bush plan for Iraq: that 'our mistake was to put ourselves in a corner so quickly. Our challenge is now to find a graceful way out of a box of our own making' (to the US Senate, 12 February 2003, cited in the *Guardian*, 18 February 2003, p. 17).
40 Robin Cook, resignation speech to the House of Commons, 18 March 2003.
41 It was very noticeable, throughout the build-up to the invasion, that it was the UK Government, not the Bush Administration, that was making the running on the Israeli-Palestinian link to the Iraqi crisis. When in London in November 2001, standing next to Tony Blair, President Bush was asked explicitly about the linkage – about whether al-Qaeda could be defeated 'without a Middle East settlement' – he replied: 'Oh, I believe we can. I believe we're going to.' Then he added, as an afterthought: 'Having said that, however, we are both working hard to try to bring peace to the Middle East.' Tony Blair, by contrast, was always clear that, as part of its response to the events of 9/11, the UK was totally committed to the creation of 'a secure Israel, confident in its security' and 'a Palestinian state with justice for the Palestinian people' (press conference given by Prime Minister Tony Blair to Arab journalists, 19 October 2001).
42 For a representative case of this, see 'Egyptian intellectual speaks of the Arab world's despair', *New York Times*, 8 April 2003, p. B1.
43 Jimmy Carter, 'Just war, or a just war?', *New York Times*, 9 March 2003.
44 Cited in B. Herbert, 'The art of the false impression', *New York Times*, 11 August 2003.

45 NBC News-Wall Street Journal poll, *New York Times*, 30 July 2003.

46 'Blair says Britons unconvinced on Iraq', *New York Times*, 30 July 2003.

47 This is quite a story in its own right: as sequentially the buck was passed to British intelligence, to the CIA, to Condoleezza Rice's deputy and then Rice herself, and finally to the President, who on 30 July took 'full personal responsibility for everything I say' (on this, see the transcript of his 30 July press conference, and 'Bush denies claim he oversold the war', *New York Times*, 31 July 2003).

48 It also raised a serious double standard. By late July the UK Government found itself accused by sections of the British press of having 'blood on its hands' because of the death of David Kelly. No such accusations, however, were made, or those that were never came with the same intensity, when the press turned to the question of military casualties (both coalition and Iraqi) or civilian casualties (entirely Iraqi). Counting bodies was very selectively done by the US and UK press core throughout this whole tragic set of events.

49 George Bush, 6 September 2003.

50 George Bush, to the UN Security Council, 23 September 2003.

51 Quoted in the *New York Times*, 25 July 2003, p. A10.

52 Colin Powell on CNN's Late Edition, 28 September 2003.

53 Oral evidence, the Prime Minister to the Liaison Committee, 8 July 2003.

54 Oral evidence, the Foreign Secretary to the Committee, 27 June 2003.

55 In fact, Jack Straw became particularly adept over time at the art of squaring circles in this fashion. So when the preliminary report of the Iraq Survey Group was issued in October 2003, indicating their total failure to find weapons of mass destruction, Robin Cook understandably hailed that finding as evidence that the policy of containment had worked. Not so Jack Straw: he felt the findings that there were no weapons of mass destruction actually justified an invasion predicated on their insistence, because in his view, without the invasion, Saddam Hussein would have expelled the inspectors and renewed weapon construction. He told the BBC this: 'If we had not taken military action at the time we did, in the face of that defiance, then the resolve of the international community would have died down, and then inspectors would have found it more and more difficult to do their work as they had done before. Then they would have been kicked out. Then we would have had a Saddam Hussein still there, re-empowered and re-emboldened and able to develop these programmes in a more dangerous form, to continue to disrupt the region and threaten international peace and security and continue his reign of terror on his own people' (*Guardian*, 3 October 2003). You have to admire the creativity, not to mention the cheek, of a perennially sliding defence of this kind.

56 This last from US Assistant Secretary of State John Bolton, in claiming that 'the issue was not weapons or actual programs, but the capability that Iraq sought to have . . . WMD programs. Saddam . . . kept a coterie

of scientists he was preserving for the day when he could build nuclear weapons unhindered by international constraints. Whether he possessed them today or four years ago isn't really the issue. . . . As long as that regime was in power, it was determined to get nuclear, chemical and biological weapons one way or another. Until that regime was removed from power, that threat remained – that was the purpose of the military action' (cited in the *Independent*, 7 September 2003).

57   Quoted on the website of BBC News, 14 and 15 July, 2003.
58   Oral evidence, the Foreign Secretary to the Committee, 27 June 2003.
59   House of Commons Foreign Affairs Committee, *The Decision to go to War in Iraq* (The Stationery Office Ltd, 7 July 2003), paragraph 30.

CHAPTER 6   MOTIVES AND WORLD VIEWS

1   Tony Blair, 'The left should not weep if Saddam is toppled', *Guardian*, 10 February 2003.
2   See 'America's democratic imperialists', *Financial Times*, 6 March 2003, p. 11.
3   On this, see F. Keane, 'The road to war', in BBC News, *The Battle for Baghdad* (London: BBC, 2003), p. 44.
4   For a detailed account of New Labour–BP ties, see David Osler, *Labour Party PLC: New Labour as a Party of Business* (Edinburgh and London: Mainstream Publishing, 2002), pp. 202–4. We are grateful to Tom Ferguson for drawing our attention to the New Labour–BP links and for recommending this source.
5   Nat Irwin, 'Reason: light dawns about why we fought', *Winston-Salem Journal*, 8 June 2003, p. A21. Thomas Friedman's *New York Times* op-ed piece of 4 June 2003 agreed: 'The real reason for this war', he wrote, 'which was never really stated, was that after 9/11 America needed to hit someone in the Arab-Muslim world [and] Afghanistan wasn't enough.' To prove to radical Muslims that the USA hadn't gone soft, as they claimed, it was vital, according to Friedman, 'for American soldiers . . . to go into the heart of the Arab-Muslim world, house to house, and make clear that we are ready to kill, and to die, to prevent our open society from being undermined by . . . terrorism. . . . If you talk to US soldiers in Iraq they will tell you this is what the war is about.'
6   Tony Blair, 'The left should not weep if Saddam is toppled', *Guardian*, 10 February 2003.
7   *Guardian*, 3 October 2001, p. 5.
8   See for example, Philip Webster, *The Times*, 3 May 2003.
9   P. Stothard, *30 Days: A Month at the Heart of Blair's War* (London: Harper-Collins, 2003), p. 87.
10   Martin Kettle, 'America wanted war', *Guardian*, 16 July 2003, p. 19.
11   More generally on this way of understanding Labour politics, see D. Coates, 'Strategic choices in the study of New Labour', *British Journal of Politics and International Relations*, 4, 3 (October 2002): 479–86.

12 See Philippe Schmitter, 'Still the century of corporatism?', *Review of Politics*, 36, 1 (1974): 85–131; John H. Goldthorpe (ed.), *Order and Conflict in Contemporary Capitalism: Studies in the Political Economy of Western European Nations* (Oxford: Oxford University Press, 1984).

13 Geoffrey Foote, *The Labour Party's Political Thought: A History*, 3rd edn (New York: St Martin's Press, 1997), p. 13.

14 David Coates, *The Labour Party and the Struggle for Socialism* (London: Cambridge University Press, 1975), pp. 136–40.

15 Eric Shaw, *The Labour Party Since 1945* (Oxford: Blackwell Publishers, 1996), p. 44.

16 Bruce George, *The British Labour Party and Defense* (New York: Praeger, 1991), p. 9.

17 Michael R. Gordon, *Conflict and Consensus in Labour's Foreign Policy, 1914–1965* (Stanford, CA: Stanford University Press, 1969), p. 1.

18 See David Coates, Gordon Johnston and Ray Bush (eds), *A Socialist Anatomy of Britain* (Cambridge: Polity, 1985), p. 199.

19 Cited in Peter Hennessy, *Never Again: Britain, 1945–1951* (New York: Pantheon Books, 1993), p. 233.

20 Ibid., p. 268. See also Shaw, *The Labour Party Since 1945*, pp. 19–49.

21 Stephen Haseler, *The Tragedy of Labour* (Oxford: Basil Blackwell, 1980), p. 25.

22 See John J. Mearsheimer, *The Tragedy of Great Power Politics* (New York and London: Norton, 2001), pp. 234–66.

23 See George, *The British Labour Party and Defense*, pp. 29–39.

24 Cited in ibid., p. 10.

25 See C. A. R. Crosland, *The Future of Socialism* (New York: Schocken Books, 1963).

26 See Coates et al., *A Socialist Anatomy of Britain*, p. 261.

27 Gordon, *Conflict and Consensus*, p. 24.

28 Cited in ibid., p. 6.

29 Ibid., pp. 15–16.

30 Ibid., pp. 13–44.

31 Foote, *The Labour Party's Political Thought*, p. 262.

32 Gordon, *Conflict and Consensus*, pp. 18–183.

33 Foote, *The Labour Party's Political Thought*, p. 286.

34 Peter Mandelson and Roger Liddle, *The Blair Revolution: Can New Labour Deliver?* (London: Faber and Faber, 1996), p. 27.

35 Labour Party, 1997 General Election Manifesto, *New Labour, Because Britain Deserves Better*, p. 15.

36 Ibid., p. 2 (Tony Blair's introduction).

37 Ibid., p. 15.

38 Mearsheimer, *The Tragedy of Great Power Politics*. Like Mearsheimer's 'offensive realism', our 'offensive multilateralism' emphasizes the strategic choice to shift the balance of power by aggressively advancing national interests in a world thought to lack authoritative global institutions.

39 Desmond King and Mark Wickham-Jones, 'Training without the state? New Labour and labour markets', *Politics and Society*, 26, 4 (1998): 439–55.
40 Tony Blair, Lecture at the commemoration organized by the Fabian Society to mark the fiftieth anniversary of the 1945 General Election (London: Labour Party, 1995).
41 Norman Fairclough, *New Labour, New Language?* (London and New York: Routledge, 2000), p. 148. The discussion of Blair's 'Doctrine of the international community' that follows was inspired by Fairclough's very useful analysis.
42 Tony Blair, 'Doctrine of the international community', speech to the Economic Club of Chicago, Hilton Hotel, Chicago, Thursday 22 April 1999.
43 Ibid.
44 Ibid.
45 Ibid. In that speech, Blair laid out five tests against which to decide whether or not to intervene: 'first, are we sure of our case . . . second, have we exhausted all diplomatic options . . . third . . . are there military operations we can sensibly and prudently undertake . . . fourth, are we prepared for the long term . . . And finally, do we have national interests involved?'
46 Ibid.

CHAPTER 7 REFLECTIONS AND LESSONS

1 Paul Wolfowitz, in a prepared statement for the House and Senate Armed Services Committees, 3 and 4 October 2001.
2 Paul Wolfowitz, speaking to the International Institute for Strategic Studies, London, 2 December 2002.
3 *The National Security Strategy of the United States*, September 2002, pp. 13–15.
4 In his introduction to the NSS document, p. 1.
5 On this key confusion, see later, pp. 149–51.
6 *The National Security Strategy of the United States*, p. 15.
7 Ibid., p. 13.
8 P. Krugman, 'Denial and deception', *New York Times*, 24 June 2003, p. A31.
9 To quote *The New Republic*: 'Had the Administration accurately depicted the consensus within the intelligence community in 2002 – that Iraq's ties with al-Qaeda were inconsequential; that its nuclear weapons program was minimal at best; and that its chemical and biological weapons program, which had yielded significant stocks of dangerous weapons in the past, may or may not have been on-going – it would have had a very difficult time convincing Congress and the American public to support a war to disarm Saddam. But the Bush Administration painted a very different, and a far more frightening, picture'

(S. Ackerman and J. B. Judis, 'The first casualty', *The New Republic*, 30 June 2003, p. 15).

10 The US and UK Governments might just have been able to square this particular circle if their arms sales policies were subject to tight ethical rules. It was this that Robin Cook tried to do for the UK after 1997, and at which he failed. The *Guardian* reported, just a month before the invasion, that, on the contrary, the UK Government was now supplying arms to countries with poor human rights records – countries such as Uzbekistan, Turkmenistan and Kyrgyzstan – because these countries bordered Afghanistan and were therefore useful allies in the fight against terrorism. (See Richard Norton Taylor, 'Export of arms criticised', *Guardian*, 27 February 2003, p. 12.) Cook's problem here underscores the degree to which New Labour's ethical ambitions in the area of *foreign* policy required a much wider resetting of UK *domestic* policies and structures: a resetting that New Labour has yet to recognize, let alone confront. It is very hard to be ethical in foreign policy and a major arms dealer at one and the same time.

11 Health experts at the University of Columbia, in a study commissioned by the US Government, reported in April 2003 that between 1961 and 1971 the US military sprayed more than 77 million litres of Agent Orange on parts of what is now southern Vietnam, that 'millions of Vietnamese were likely to have been sprayed upon directly', and that in consequence some Vietnamese today still have 200 times the normal levels of dioxin in their bodies.

12 The US track record here since 1945 is not great: supporting democratic overthrows and repressive military dictatorships in Iran, Guatemala, South Vietnam, Chile, Indonesia, Saudi Arabia, Cambodia and Zaire; and funding 'freedom fighters' in Nicaragua, El Salvador, Colombia, Argentina, Angola, Mozambique – the list is a very long and dark one.

13 The June 2003 Pew survey of 21 nations showed a deepening scepticism towards the USA. 'The war had widened the rift between Americans and Western Europeans, further inflamed the Muslim world, softened support for the war on terrorism, and significantly weakened global public support for the pillars of the post World War II era – the UN and the North Atlantic alliance', according to Pew's director (quoted in the *New York Times*, 4 June 2003). Pew found that the percentage of its national samples in Middle Eastern countries expressing support for the US (already low) fell between mid-2002 and June 2003 from 35 to 27 in the Lebanon, 25 to 1 in Jordan and 14 to 1 in the Palestinian Authority (*Financial Times*, 4 June 2003, p. 2).

14 See, for example, President Bush, addressing the American Enterprise Institute, 27 February 2003.

15 *The Economist*, 24 May 2003, p. 57.

16 On the general origins of the post-1970s 'Islamic resurgence', see S. Huntington, *The Clash of Civilizations and the Remaking of World Order* (New York: Simon and Schuster, 1996), pp. 109–20.

17 Marc Racicot, for the Republican National Committee, fund-raising circular, April 2003.

18 Peter Stothard discusses the role of Blair and Bush's religious convictions in this regard (*30 Days: A Month at the Heart of Blair's War* (London: Harper-Collins, 2003), p. 40).

19 On this, see Bob Woodward, *Bush At War* (New York: Simon and Schuster, 2002), p. 63.

20 Tony Blair was actually quizzed on this at the Liaison Committee. Asked if the remarks made by Hillary Clinton in London about the role of 'neo-cons' in US foreign policy-making tempted him to change his attitude to standing 'shoulder to shoulder' with the USA, he said that they did not. Insisting that the UK makes its own policy and that the alliance on Iraq was based on 'the threat to do with terrorism and WMD', he told the Committee that he did not care if beliefs about that threat 'came from so-called "neo-cons" or comes from so-called "liberals". I am not from that part of the political spectrum myself, but I do genuinely believe [terrorism] is a huge threat' (oral evidence, 28 July 2003).

21 It is significant in this regard that chapter 6 of the September 2002 document, *The National Security Strategy of the United States*, should be titled 'Ignite a new era of global economic growth through free markets and free trade'; and that the USA has recently signed a free trade agreement with Jordan and is advocating similar agreements across the Middle East.

22 An influential commission led by Willy Brandt, former Chancellor of the Federal Republic of Germany, analysed the challenges that would confront the global economy from the early 1980s through to the end of the century. The Brandt Report called for a fundamental restructuring of the global economy to reduce the development gap between North and South, criticized the role of the developed countries in controlling the institutions and rules that governed international finance and trade, and recommended that emergency measures be taken to alleviate poverty in the developing world.

23 *Guardian*, 19 August 2003, p. 1.

24 Ibid., 13 September 2003, p. 1.

25 Tony Blair, 'I want to go faster and further', speech to the Labour Party conference, 30 September 2003.

26 Cited in P. Wintour, 'Ministers round on Cook over diaries serialization', *Guardian*, 6 October 2003. The Cook diaries were published by Simon and Schuster in October 2003 under the title *Point of Departure*.

27 Cited in W. Hoge, 'Blair doubted Iraq had arms, ex-aide says', *New York Times*, 6 October 2003.

28 See, for example, N. Cohen, 'The Left isn't listening', *Observer*, 16 February 2003, p. 31; and for a fine rebuttal, Jonathan Freedland, 'What would you suggest?' *Guardian*, 19 February 2003, p. 17.

29 'Reality Check', *The New Republic*, 30 June 2003, p. 7.

30 Oral evidence, Liaison Committee, 28 July 2003.

CHAPTER 8   TOWARDS AN ETHICAL FOREIGN POLICY

1   'Speech of Edmund Burke, esq., on Moving His Resolutions for Conciliation with the Colonies, March 22, 1775', in *Select Works of Edmund Burke*, vol. 1 (Indianapolis: Liberty Fund, 1999), p. 236. The authors are grateful to Debra Candreva and Edward Stettner for their efforts in locating the source of Boyce's quotation from Burke.

2   Michael Boyce, 'Achieving effect: annual Chief of Defense Staff Lecture', *RUSI Journal*, 148, 1 (February 2003): 31–7.

3   Michael Boyce, 'UK strategic choices following the Strategic Defense Review and 11th September', *RUSI Journal*, 147, 1 (February 2002): 3.

4   Boyce, 'Achieving effect', p. 35.

5   Michael Boyce, 'UK strategic choices', p. 4.

6   George W. Bush, 'Statement by the President in his address to the nation', the White House, Office of the Press Secretary, 11 September 2001.

7   Michael Walzer, 'First define the battlefield', *New York Times*, 21 September 2001, p. A35.

8   Michael Howard, 'What's in a name? How to fight terrorism,' *Foreign Affairs*, 81, 1 (2002): 9.

9   That others outside the United States instinctively embraced the perspective that 9/11 was first and foremost an attack on America was captured by the instantly famous observation by Jean-Marie Colombani in the 12 September copy of *Le Monde*: 'In this tragic moment, when words seem so inadequate to express the shock people feel, the first thing that comes to mind is this: We are all Americans! We are all New Yorkers.' But like John F. Kennedy's June 1963 declaration, 'I am a Berliner', evoked by the *Le Monde* article, post-9/11 expressions of solidarity are anchored in a broader context. For Kennedy, a Cold War appeal for freedom and democracy in Berlin and in Germany was explicitly linked to a broader effort to secure stability in Europe and, beyond that, to advance 'a peaceful and hopeful globe'. Similarly, the 12 September statement by NATO's North American Council invoked Article 5 of the Washington Treaty to confirm that the attacks on America were an attack against all NATO countries. In the same vein, the Security Council Resolution passed on the same day unmistakably established the broader context, declaring the attacks in New York, Washington, DC and Pennsylvania 'a threat to international peace and security'.

10   Michael Reisman, 'In defense of world public order', *The American Journal of International Law*, 95, 4 (October 2001): 833.

11   Jonathan I. Charney, 'The use of force against terrorism and international law', *The American Journal of International Law*, 95, 4 (October 2001): 835–9.

12   Tariq Modood, 'Muslims in the West', *Observer*, 30 September 2001.

13   George W. Bush, 'Statement by the President in his address to the nation', The White House, Office of the Press Secretary, 11 September 2001.

14   See Neta C. Crawford, 'Just war theory and the US counter-terror war', *APSA Perspectives on Politics*, 1, 1 (March 2003): 5–25.
15   Frederic Megret, 'War? Legal semantics and the move to violence', *European Journal of International Law*, 13, 2 (2002): 361.
16   J. A. Paul, 'Security Council reform: Arguments about the future of the United Nations system'; available at <http://www/globalpolicy.org/security/pubs/secref.htm>
17   Niel Blokker, 'Is the authorization authorized? Powers and practice of the UN Security Council to authorize the use of force by "coalitions of the able and willing"', *European Journal of International Law*, 11, 3 (2000): 541.
18   Ibid., p. 543.
19   International Commission on Intervention and State Sovereignty, *The Responsibility To Protect: Report of the International Commission on Intervention and State Sovereignty*, December 2001.
20   Richard Falk, 'After Iraq is there a future for the charter system? War prevention and the UN', *Counterpunch*, 2 July 2003.
21   'Adoption of policy of pre-emption could result in proliferation of unilateral, lawless use of force, Secretary General tells General Assembly', September 2003.
22   Blokker, 'Is the authorization authorized?', p. 541.
23   C. Brown, 'Self-defense in an imperfect world', *Ethics and International Affairs*, 17, 1 (2003): 5.
24   For a related argument, see Falk, 'After Iraq is there a future for the charter system?'
25   Robert Keohane, 'A credible promise to the United Nations', *Financial Times*, 31 March 2003.
26   Brown, 'Self-defense in an imperfect world', p. 5.
27   Jürgen Habermas, 'Interpreting the fall of a monument', *German Law Journal*, 4, 7 (1 July 2003).
28   Ibid.
29   See: Thomas M. Franck, 'Lessons of Kosovo', *The American Journal of International Law*, 93, 4 (October 1999): 857–60; Richard A. Falk, 'Kosovo, world order, and the future of international law', *The American Journal of International Law*, 93, 4 (October 1999): 847–57.
30   Falk, 'After Iraq is there a future for the charter system?'
31   Franck, 'Lessons of Kosovo', pp. 857–60.
32   See, for example, Jonathan I. Charney, 'Anticipatory humanitarian intervention in Kosovo', *The American Journal of International Law*, 93, 4 (October 1999): 834–41. The discussion of the burden of proof that follows is influenced by Charney's argument, although it departs from it in a number of ways. There are similarities here too with the five tests for intervention outlined by Tony Blair in his Chicago 1999 speech. Our view is that our requirements are more demanding than his; and that his policy in Iraq failed to meet even his own Chicago tests.
33   See Falk, 'After Iraq is there a future for the charter system?'

34 Progressive Governance Summit, 13–14 July 2003 Communiqué, available at <http://www.number-10.gov.uk/output/page4146.asp>

35 Tony Blair, 'Doctrine of the international community', speech to the Economic Club of Chicago, Hilton Hotel, Chicago, Thursday 22 April 1999.

36 Michael Walzer, *Just and Unjust Wars*, 3rd edn (New York: Basic Books, 2000), pp. 74–5.

37 Ministry of Defence, *The Strategic Defence Review: A New Chapter*, July 2002, Cm5566, vol. I, 2.2, 'Prevention', pp. 10–11.

38 Richard K. Betts, 'Striking first: A history of thankfully lost opportunities', *Ethics and International Affairs*, 17, 1 (2003): 18.

39 George W. Bush, 'Remarks by the President at 2002 graduation exercise of the United States Military Academy, West Point, New York', 1 June 2002.

40 *The National Security Strategy of the United States of America*, September 2002.

41 Ibid.

42 Ibid.

43 Walzer, *Just and Unjust Wars*, p. 76.

44 Betts, 'Striking first', p. 18.

45 Walzer, *Just and Unjust Wars*, p. 77.

46 Betts, 'Striking first', p. 21.

Index

9/11 attacks, *see under* terrorism, international